D0295516

BAKE &
decorate
TEA TIME LUXURY

FIONA CAIRNS

photographs by Laura Hynd

Quadrille
PUBLISHING

For Kishore, Hari and Tara, with my love.
Thanks for giving me your summer.

WILTSHIRE LIBRARIES	
5134272000	
Bertrams	16/03/2010
641.8653	£19.99
	01010596

Baking and eating cakes and biscuits is all about home, comfort, pleasure and luxury. Admittedly, they are not an essential part of our daily diet or sustenance, but they are vital to our souls. Cakes are a treat. They can be a gift, an occasion in their own right to be shared while relaxing around a kitchen table, eaten indulgently solo, or given as a centrepiece at a lavish celebration with loved ones. For me, they are also about the unmistakeable sweet aroma of the oven, the light texture of a cake crumb or the tantalising fragrance of citrus and rosewater in a syrup.

Cakes create memories. I'd like our children to have those memories, too. For many of us, baking was our first introduction to the kitchen and I remember fighting over scraping down and licking the mixing bowl with my brother. Even now, I have been known to sneak the last of some silky, melted, still-warm chocolate. Sadly, in our increasingly busy lives, many of us these days lack the time and knowledge to bake. I want to change that. I hope to show in this book that the process of baking and decorating is just as enjoyable as the eating; it might surprise you. Everyone makes mistakes, even the professionals, so a lack of confidence is no reason not to give it a try. Once, when making Christmas cakes, I lost an earring in the batter. I only found it with the help of a metal detector!

You will find some very simple recipes in this book clearly explained, which you can decorate or not, depending on your mood and the occasion. If this is all new to you, try something easy at first – maybe a Victoria Sponge, or one of my recipes that require no cooking, such as sumptuous Gilded Chocolate Tiffin – and progress from there.

Baking differs from other types of cookery because it really is all about exact measurements, basic rules and oven temperatures. This means you do need to follow the recipes in the Bake chapter closely. All of them will stand you in excellent stead for the rest of your baking life ahead. You may find new, sophisticated favourites, such as my exotic, headily scented Star Anise, Almond and Clementine Syrup Cake, or turn to the warmth of classics such as an impeccable Battenberg. All the recipes work perfectly; once you have followed the instructions, you will always have a successful and delicious cake that tastes wonderful. Don't worry; that's the bossy bit over now!

The creations in the Decorate chapter – all made from my Bake recipes – are there to spark your own imagination. They are intended as a starting point. If I have inspired you to try some of the ideas or, even better, to find new ways to express your own creativity, and you find yourself wondering what to try next, then I have succeeded. Do also have a look at my 25 Easy Cheats, which will help you to conjure up a fabulous cake with a minimum of fuss, cost or effort.

Cake decorating can seem daunting, but this book is certainly not. There are no hard-to-follow steps or long, scary lists of equipment. Many of the decorated cakes require little special kit, previous knowledge or masses of time. Some use the everyday objects we are surrounded with, such as baked bean cans, ribbons or fresh flowers, in imaginative ways. They will let you rediscover the ancient pleasures to be had from crafting something beautiful with your hands.

As you improve in confidence and skill, your reputation will grow. You'll become the best host in town for glamorous tea parties – or decadent soirees – the nurturing homemaker and the mainstay, relied upon to make a stunning cake with elegance, glamour and charm.

Mothers will find new ways to lift a child's birthday party into a wild success; try making quirky Flying Insect cakes, or even bake delightful Ice-cream Cones, cakes that won't melt in the sun.

If tea parties are more your thing, hold a spring celebration with a White Chocolate, Cardamom and Rosewater Sponge that will have guests clamouring for the recipe, or produce a table laden with Doily Biscuits, Sticky Ginger Cake and Chocolate Chilli Cupcakes to bring comfort to a winter afternoon. Just make sure you offer something a little stronger alongside the pots of tea.

Whatever your style, my book will help you achieve the perfect, most delicious occasion for your friends and family, where the cake is the star and the baker glows in its reflected warmth. Happy baking!

ingredients

As in all cooking, the better the ingredients, the more delicious the results, so do not stint. Buy the best you can afford.

butter
I use unsalted butter and so do these recipes. The exception is where I specify salted butter, such as for my Classic Shortbread (see p74). I never use margarine. Margarine gives a light cake, as it has already been whipped, but if you follow my instructions for creaming butter you will have a feather-light cake with a far superior flavour.

chocolate
This subject is a minefield. These days we're faced with an array of high-quality chocolates with varying percentages and it can be daunting. The percentage indicates the amount of cocoa solids in the chocolate. In these recipes I indicate the best sort to use. Where I specify milk chocolate, use a bar with at least 30% cocoa solids. With white chocolate buy good Swiss bars, which I find most successful for cooking and making ganaches.

citrus
Use unwaxed lemons where available, especially if you are using the zest.

dulche de leche
A delicious caramel sauce from Argentina, found in jars in most supermarkets.

eggs
Do use organic or free-range eggs. I use large, and all the recipes in this book assume you do, too.

flour
I use unbleached flour as I find it has more flavour, it is purer and free from chemicals; use traditional stoneground flour if possible.

nuts
Buy little and often, as they turn rancid very quickly. Please make a point of roasting them, as I suggest; it makes a huge difference as it releases their oils. Any leftover nuts freeze brilliantly.

rosewater and orange flower water
Widely available from supermarkets, but try to buy from a Middle Eastern shop if you can, as the fragrance is more intense (so use a smaller amount).

spices
Buy small amounts and store them in the dark. Please buy whole nutmegs and freshly grate them as needed; the flavour is incomparable to pre-ground.

sugar
Unrefined sugar has much more flavour; do try to use golden caster sugar instead of white (except for snowy white meringues). Muscovado sugars are quite delicious; their taste and colour comes from the molasses clinging to the grains. Light muscovado has a butterscotch flavour and creams very well. Dark muscovado requires a little more care - it is a strong flavour that could easily overpower - but its delicious treacly taste is perfect in rich fruit cakes. If it goes rock hard (as it will if the packet is left open to the air), empty it into an ovenproof dish, cover with foil and soften in a very low oven.

sugarpaste
This makes covering and decorating cakes so easy. It is widely available, and I don't think it's worth making yourself. Once kneaded, sugarpaste becomes pliable and gives cakes a lovely smooth finish. It is great for forming shapes, too; a bit like children's modelling clay. It comes in a range of colours, but I prefer to mix my own more interesting shades.

treacle and syrup
Far easier to measure if you first oil the measuring spoon, or dip it into boiling water.

vanilla
Use only pure vanilla extract, or vanilla pods. Always avoid anything labelled 'vanilla flavour', as it is synthetic and doesn't taste at all like the real thing. A good habit to get into is to make vanilla sugar. Stick 3–4 vanilla pods into a jar of caster sugar and leave for a week or two. Top up as required. This is invaluable for baking or sprinkling on to shortbreads, cakes and fruits.

equipment

baking parchment
I use non-stick baking parchment for lining tins. It is essential for meringues; they will stick to greaseproof paper.

buttercream
300g unsalted butter, softened
400g icing sugar, sifted

In an electric mixer, beat the butter until really pale and fluffy. Add your flavour and the icing sugar and beat for at least 5 minutes, until light and creamy.

flavourings
vanilla 2 tsp vanilla extract or seeds of 1 vanilla pod
chocolate 100g 70% cocoa solids chocolate, melted and cooled, or 2 tbsp cocoa powder, sifted
coffee 2 tbsp strong black coffee
raspberry/blueberry/strawberry 4 tbsp fresh fruit puree (not too wet)
lemon/orange/lime zest of 2 fruits, finely grated, and juice of 1, added slowly at the end
liqueur 1 tbsp, added slowly at the end
nut 150g roasted, ground and cooled nuts

cupcake and fairy cake cases
There is an ever-increasing array on the market, and it is seriously confusing. The sizes and names vary and, therefore, will alter how many you can make in a batch and their cooking times. The instructions I have given worked for me and are approximate. As a general rule, the very small cases are called 'petit four' or 'sweet' cases. The next size up are often called 'bun' or 'fairy cake' cases, then the larger 'cupcake' and, even deeper, the largest 'muffin'.

oven
Ovens vary enormously: no 2 are the same and you are very familiar with yours. It is very useful to have an oven thermometer, to check if yours is too cool or too hot. Always preheat the oven and have the shelves at the correct heights. (It is best to bake a cake in the centre of a fan oven, or on the top shelf of a conventional oven.) This way, you won't have your cakes sitting around while you fiddle with the shelves and lose valuable heat... sound familiar?

piping bags
Here is how to make a piping bag from baking parchment for royal icing. If you prefer, you can buy them from cake decorating shops, or find tubes in the supermarket with icing and nozzle in place. Remember you'll need to buy nylon, washable bags for piping buttercream and meringues.

Start with a 30cm square of baking parchment. Fold in half to form a double-thickness triangle. Place it with the tip pointing away from you. The centre of the long side nearest you will form the tip where the icing will come out (and where you put a nozzle). Twist the parchment around to form a cone, then secure with your thumb and forefinger. Adjust the layers until you have a sharp tip. (When using more than 60g of icing, make and use a bigger bag.)

Fold all the overlapping papers inside the cone twice to secure. Cut 2 little snips 1cm apart in the folds to hold the seam, then fold back this tab. Only ever half-fill a bag, and fold shut the open end.

royal icing
1 egg white
250g icing sugar, sifted

Using an electric mixer, whisk the egg until bubbles appear. Now whisk in the sugar bit by bit. Continue to whisk for 1–2 minutes. The consistency is key; it must hold its shape when piped. Gradually add water to thin, or icing sugar to thicken.

scales and measurements
Baking is an exact science. I'm afraid you can't sling in an extra spoonful of this or that for good measure; you must weigh everything out precisely. A good set of digital scales is invaluable.

tins
There is a huge variety on the market; buy the best you can. Really good-quality tins will last many years, conduct heat well and won't warp. Non-stick, loose-bottomed or springform tins make baking so much easier. Try to use the size of tin specified. If you don't have the correct size, err on the side of a slightly larger tin (the cake will be shallower) and reduce the baking time by 5–10 minutes.

baking tips

As I have said in the ingredients section (see p8), once you have good-quality components, you're halfway there!

read the recipe
Always read right to the end and only then assemble all the ingredients and equipment you need. This makes life easier, less stressful and more enjoyable.

temperature of mixing bowls and ingredients
A warm kitchen, equipment and ingredients make a great cake. So, when baking a cake, stand your mixing bowl and beater or whisk in a bowl of warm water, then dry thoroughly before you start. Conversely, cooler ingredients and temperatures result in perfect biscuits. Hence, marble and cold hands are good for biscuit making. Is this why Scottish shortbreads are so famous?
Try to think ahead and remove eggs and butter from the refrigerator the night before. But, if the urge to bake suddenly strikes, stand the eggs in a bowl of warm water, and blitz the butter in the microwave.

creaming butter and sugar
I have usually suggested 5 minutes to cream the butter and sugar - both for a cake and for buttercream - and, should you time yourself, you will see it is quite a while. The reason is that there is a very noticeable difference: the colour changes and the mixture becomes aerated as it increases in volume, turning paler and fluffy. Keep scraping the sides of your bowl with a spatula during the process to make sure all ingredients are well blended in.

light as air
When sifting flour, lift the sieve up high; this allows air to coat the particles of flour as they float down.

lining tins
If tins are of good quality and have been well buttered, the sides do not need to be lined. The exception is if you're baking a cake that will be in the oven a long time (such as a fruit cake), when it will help protect the sides. If at all in doubt, line the sides with baking parchment too.

don't hang around ...
Once a cake's in the tin, put it into the oven immediately as, when moist, the raising agents start to work. (A dense fruit cake batter isn't so sensitive.)

...but be patient!
Don't be tempted to open the oven door to peep at your cake too often. Leave this until the final 5–10 minutes. If you keep opening the door at the start, you will affect the rise and texture of the cake.

when is it ready?
Insert a thin skewer into the very centre of your cake. If it emerges clean, the cake is cooked. Long-baked fruit cakes may need extra attention: cut a piece of foil to fit the surface. Pierce a hole in the centre and open it up. This lets out steam while protecting the surface from drying out or scorching.

disaster management
—You only need to lose the bottom half of a sticky or fragile cake to a wire rack once; in future, you'll place a sheet of baking parchment on first.
—If your cake isn't cooked in the middle or has sunk, all is not lost. Dig out and discard the middle then fill the resulting hole with cream and berries.
—On New Year's Eve (after the shops shut) I made a very large rich chocolate cake for a party. I took it too soon from the oven; it was raw inside. So I cut out rounds (avoiding the centre), decorated with gold leaf and arranged on a platter. No one knew.
—When adding eggs to creamed butter and sugar, do so very slowly, as the batter can otherwise curdle. If it does, just carry on. The cake may not rise as it should, but will taste delicious.
—If your cake is very dry, douse it with a dessert or fortified wine and use it as the base for a trifle.

a note on perfect biscuits
When rolling out, cut the shapes as close together as possible so you are not re-rolling too often (or the dough will toughen). When ready, biscuits will look darker but may seem underdone. They aren't. They will crisp up. Always space biscuits out on the baking sheet at least 1cm apart, as they spread.

decorating tips

sculpting and shaping
If cutting up a cake, a short spell (1 hour) in the refrigerator or freezer makes it easier to shape.

icing
be generous You'll always need more marzipan or sugarpaste; start with the amounts specified.
cool it Always make sure the cake is absolutely cold, or it will be soggy and the icing will not stick.

get the foundations right
Turn the cake upside down so the base becomes a flat top. Cracks or blemishes can be filled in with buttercream, sugarpaste or marzipan.

sugarpaste
Knead to make it pliable and, if it is too sticky, dust your hands and work surface with icing sugar. If it dries, add a tiny amount of white vegetable fat. Use a food processor with a dough hook, as it saves your muscles. Store in a sealed polythene bag at room temperature (never the refrigerator).
When rolling it out, dust a dry work surface and rolling pin with icing sugar and be sure frequently to run a palette knife underneath. It's very frustrating if it sticks to the surface. Never store a sugarpaste-covered cake or decorations in the refrigerator. When covering a cake, ensure your rolled-out sugarpaste is slightly larger than the cake and sides, and wrap it loosely around the rolling pin before smoothing it on to the cake. If there are air bubbles, prick them with a pin and rub away the hole.
Once a cake is covered, store in a cardboard box, not an airtight container as it will sweat. Avoid contact with water, which will mark it.

colouring sugarpaste
Colour the sugarpaste the day before you need it, as it will be easier to roll and mould. Dip the end of a fine skewer into food colour paste and drag it across the sugarpaste. Knead until it's an even colour and you achieve the desired shade. If you need different tones, make the darker first then lighten with white sugarpaste, or it's hard to get the same shade. With strong colours, wear gloves to protect your hands.

food colour
Use food colour paste, not liquid, where you can. In either case, food colours can be a little unsubtle, so mix them up for a more interesting palette. A pinprick of brown, even black, works wonders. They are intense, so you'll only need a very small amount.

adding ribbons
Stick ribbons with a dab of icing at the back only, as it will dry to leave a mark which should be hidden.

hiding flaws
Many designs in this book are very forgiving. Any blemishes can be covered with a decoration.

transporting decorated cakes
Cakes are more robust than you may think and most transport easily. When taking a cake to a venue, err on the side of caution and take a repair kit - a bag of royal icing and a few spare decorations - in the rare event that something has fallen off or broken. It is really important that cakes are stored in dry conditions at room temperature.

cutting a fruit cake
There's an art to cutting fruit cake, as it can crumble. Use a very sharp or serrated knife. Place the knife right across the cake and, with a gentle sawing action, cut into slices. Wipe the blade between each cut with kitchen towel. The knife won't become sticky and the icing will remain clean.

a note on freezing
As a rule, a cake is at its best freshly baked, although many will keep well for a few days and fruit cakes need time to mature.
After one of the shoots for this book, I took the Rose Garden Cake (see p109) to my neighbour, in its full finery, adorned with crystallised roses. She told me later that she had frozen the whole cake (roses and all) for the weekend. I must have sounded sceptical, as she brought the remains for me to see; she and her family found the cake delicious and the roses were intact. I write this because, although I am not keen on freezing cakes, it seems it can work!

bake

chocolate celebration cake

This is a really dark chocolate cake, perfect for a big occasion. It's also moist enough to serve as a dessert with crème fraiche and berries. This is a large amount of cake but, for a smaller party, use exactly half the recipe to fill a 23cm diameter, 7.5cm deep, round tin and bake for just 25–35 minutes.

Lightly butter a 30cm diameter, 7.5cm deep, round springform tin and line the base with baking parchment. Preheat the oven to 170°C/fan 160°C/340°F/gas mark 3½.

Set a large heatproof bowl over a saucepan of very gently simmering water, making sure the base of the bowl does not touch the water. Dissolve the coffee in 4 tbsp hot water. Add the coffee, chocolate, sugar and butter to the bowl and melt together. Cool a little, then add the flour and mix well until smooth. Tip in the egg yolks, 1 at a time, mixing between each addition.

Whisk the egg whites with the salt to stiff peaks. Using a large spoon or spatula, fold a big spoonful of egg whites into the chocolate mixture. Once combined, fold in the rest. Tip into the tin, smooth the top and bake for 40–45 minutes, or until firm to the touch and a skewer inserted into the centre comes out clean. The sides will just be beginning to shrink from the tin.

Remove from the oven, leave in the tin for about 5 minutes, then turn out on to a wire rack to cool completely.

For the ganache, melt the chocolate, cream and butter in a bowl set over very gently simmering water, again ensuring the base of the bowl does not touch the water. Stir until smooth, then cool a little to thicken before pouring over the cake. Allow to set for at least 2 hours.

SERVES 16–20

FOR THE CAKE
300g unsalted butter, cubed, plus more for the tin
4 tsp instant coffee
400g 70% cocoa solids chocolate, broken into pieces
280g golden caster sugar
120g self-raising flour, sifted
10 eggs, separated
½ tsp salt

FOR THE GANACHE
200g 70% cocoa solids chocolate, broken into pieces
100ml double cream
50g unsalted butter

TO DECORATE see: 23-carat Gold Cake, p82; Bollywood Extravaganza, p126; Chilli Chocolate Cupcakes, p167

family chocolate cake

Buttermilk helps to lighten the texture and adds flavour.

Preheat the oven to 180°C/fan 170°C/350°F/gas mark 4. Butter 2 x 20cm round sandwich tins, each 4.5cm deep, and line the bases with baking parchment.

Place the chocolate in a bowl and pour over 120ml just-boiled water. Stir until melted, then set aside to cool.

In a bowl, sift together the flour, baking powder and bicarbonate of soda, then stir in the ground almonds. In the bowl of an electric mixer (or in a bowl with a electric hand whisk), cream together the butter and sugar until very light and fluffy (this will take a good 5 minutes). Add the vanilla extract to the eggs. With the whisk running, very slowly add the egg mixture to the butter and sugar, adding 1 tbsp of the flour during the process to prevent curdling, then add the melted chocolate and the buttermilk.

Fold in the remaining flour very gently and divide the mixture between the tins. Bake for 30–35 minutes, or until firm to the touch. Leave for a minute or 2 in the tins before turning out on to a wire rack. Remove the papers and leave until absolutely cold.

To make the icing, melt the chocolate and butter in a bowl suspended over gently simmering water. Make sure the base of the bowl does not touch the water. Remove the bowl from the heat, then stir in the syrup and sugar and, lastly, gradually pour in the cream until all is well blended and smooth. Allow to cool completely, then whisk until it thickens. Spread half on the base of 1 cake. Sandwich the 2 cakes, bases together, then spread the remaining icing on top.

SERVES 8

FOR THE CAKE
175g unsalted butter, softened, plus more for the tin
100g 50–60% cocoa solids chocolate, finely chopped
200g plain flour
1 tsp baking powder
1 tsp bicarbonate of soda
100g ground almonds
275g dark muscovado sugar
1 tsp vanilla extract
3 eggs, lightly beaten
150ml buttermilk

FOR THE FUDGE ICING
90g 50–60% cocoa solids chocolate, broken into pieces
40g unsalted butter, softened and diced
1 tbsp golden syrup
2 tbsp dark muscovado sugar
150ml double cream

TO DECORATE see: Sweet Shop, p96; Party Cake with Streamers, p119; Chocolate Spiral, p144; Mint Cupcakes, p164; Parcels, p170

white chocolate and cardamom rosewater sponge

This is very delicately flavoured and the tastes of white chocolate, cardamom and rosewater marry beautifully. White chocolate ganache, which forms the filling, can be tricky. I've had my best success using Swiss white chocolate.

Preheat the oven to 180°C/fan 170°C/350°F/gas mark 4. I make this cake in a heart-shaped tin measuring 23cm at its widest point and 6.5cm deep, but otherwise use a 20cm diameter, 7.5cm deep, round tin. Butter the tin very well, then line with baking parchment.

Deseed the cardamom pods: split them with the point of a knife, empty out the little seeds and grind them to a powder in a pestle and mortar. There may be a few pieces of husk mixed in, so sift the cardamom powder together with the flour to remove them.

Place the chocolate in a food processor with half the sugar. Process until as fine as possible. Take 2 tbsp hot water - not boiling water or the chocolate will seize - and leave it until you can just dip in your finger. Dribble it into the chocolate, processing until most has melted. Add the remaining sugar and the butter, cut into knobs, and process well. Add the eggs, flour and vanilla and mix again. Don't worry if there are tiny pieces of chocolate left in the batter.

Pour into the tin and bake for 25–30 minutes or until a skewer comes out clean. Rest in the tin for a few minutes, then turn out on to a wire rack, removing the papers. Leave until absolutely cold.

Meanwhile, make the ganache. Place the chocolate in a bowl and, in a pan, bring the cream and rosewater to the boil. Pour the cream over the chocolate, leave it for a few seconds, then gently stir until smooth. Leave until cold, chill slightly, then whisk until it thickens.

Split the cake in half and invert so the flat base forms the top. Fill with the ganache and top with the second layer of cake. Place the icing sugar in a small bowl and add 1½–2 tbsp water until thick enough to coat the back of a spoon. Pour it over the cake and allow to drizzle down the sides.

TO DECORATE see: A Summer Garden, p99; Rose Petal Heart, p102

SERVES 8

FOR THE CAKE
130g unsalted butter, softened, plus more for the tin
20 green cardamom pods
170g self-raising flour
100g white chocolate, chopped
130g white caster sugar
2 eggs, beaten
1 tsp vanilla extract

FOR THE GANACHE
100g white chocolate, finely chopped
100ml double cream
2 tsp rosewater

FOR THE GLACE ICING
150g icing sugar, sifted

chocolate and beetroot cake

Beetroot is a natural dye that gives an amazing pink, and we use it a lot in the bakery. Here it stains the icing instead of the usual synthetic food colour. But, if you want an even brighter pink, cheat and add a little food colour, too. And please, whatever you do, don't use beetroot in vinegar!

Preheat the oven to 180°C/fan 170°C/350°F/gas mark 4. Lightly oil a 23cm diameter, 7.5cm deep, round tin, using a piece of kitchen towel, then line the base with baking parchment.

In a large bowl, sift together the flour, cocoa and bicarbonate of soda, then stir in the sugar. In a food processor, purée the beetroot, then scrape it into a sieve set over a bowl and push out the juices with the back of a spoon. Set them aside for the icing. Tip the beetroot pulp back into the food processor, then, with the motor running, add the eggs and vanilla, then slowly pour in the oil. Mix until blended.

Make a well in the centre of the dry ingredients, pour in the beetroot mixture and, with a large spoon, gently fold together. Pour into the tin and bake for 45–50 minutes or until a skewer inserted into the centre comes out clean. If it starts to brown too much before it is fully cooked, cut a round piece of foil the diameter of the cake, make a large hole in the centre and open it up. Place it over the cake to let out steam and protect the edges of the top surface.

Remove the cake from the oven, leave it for 5–10 minutes in the tin, then turn it out on to a wire rack until completely cold.

Sift the icing sugar into a bowl. Stir in a few drops of the reserved beetroot juice and, depending on how bright you want the colour, a little pink food colour (if you like). The icing should be thick enough to coat the back of a spoon. If not, add water, drop by drop, until you achieve the correct consistency.

Turn the cake over, so the base becomes a flat top, and spread the icing evenly over, letting it drizzle down the sides.

TO DECORATE see: Abstract Expressionist, p84

SERVES 10

FOR THE CAKE
180ml sunflower oil, plus more
    for the tin
190g self-raising flour
60g cocoa powder
1 tsp bicarbonate of soda
250g golden caster sugar
250g beetroot, cooked
3 eggs
1 tsp vanilla extract

FOR THE ICING
200g icing sugar
pink food colour (optional)

flourless chocolate hazelnut cake

For all those avoiding wheat, this is for you. Do ring the changes with the nuts, as both ground almonds or pecans would be as good as hazelnuts. If you want to try the cake as a pudding, serve it with a red fruit coulis. You can leave out the ganache if you prefer, and simply decorate the top with the raspberries dusted with icing sugar.

Preheat the oven to 180°C/fan 170°C/350°F/gas mark 4. Butter well a 20cm round cake tin, and line the base with baking parchment.

Roast the hazelnuts in the oven for 5–10 minutes, watching carefully so they don't burn, then cool and grind finely in a food processor. Place the chocolate, 70g of the sugar and the butter in a bowl set over very gently simmering water (ensure the base of the bowl does not touch the water) and melt together gently. Remove from the heat and stir in the hazelnuts. Beat the egg yolks together until they change to a paler colour, then mix them into the cooled chocolate mixture.

In another very clean bowl, whisk the egg whites, then slowly add the remaining caster sugar until the mixture forms soft peaks. Take a large spoonful and fold it into the chocolate to lighten it a little. Then fold in all the remaining egg whites, as gently and lightly as you can, using a large metal spoon or spatula. Transfer the batter to the tin and bake for about 20 minutes. This cake is fragile, so take care when handling it. Leave to cool for 10–15 minutes, then run a knife around the edge to loosen it from the tin. When the cake is cold, turn out very carefully on to a serving plate. The base will become the top.

To make the ganache, melt the chocolate, cream and butter in a bowl set over very gently simmering water (make sure the base of the bowl does not touch the water). Stir together, cool a little until it thickens, then pour it over the cake. It will be quite easy to spread with a palette knife. Stud the surface with the raspberries.

SERVES 8

FOR THE CAKE
90g unsalted butter, cubed, plus more for the tin
60g blanched hazelnuts
150g 70% cocoa solids chocolate, broken into pieces
90g golden caster sugar
3 eggs, separated

FOR THE GANACHE
100g 70% cocoa solids chocolate, broken into pieces
50ml double cream
25g unsalted butter
400g fresh raspberries

victoria sponge

This all-in-one method takes no time at all to whip up, is completely fail-safe and gives a delicious buttery sponge.

Preheat the oven to 180ºC/fan 170ºC/350ºF/gas mark 4.

You can choose to cook this cake either in 1 x 20cm sandwich tin or in 2 x 20cm sandwich tins. Butter the tin or tins, then line the bases with baking parchment. If you use just 1 tin, line the sides with a 7cm-high collar of baking parchment as well, to allow for the rise.

For this batter, I use an electric mixer and beater attachment, but use a food processor, or a bowl and an electric whisk, if you want.

Sift the flour and baking powder into the bowl, then add the butter (in knobs), the eggs, sugar and vanilla. Beat together until thoroughly blended, taking care not to over-mix so you will have a light sponge. Scrape the batter into the tin or tins and level the top.

Bake for 20–25 minutes if you are using 2 tins, or 30–35 minutes for 1 tin, until the cake springs back to the touch or a skewer inserted into the centre comes out clean.

Remove from the oven and leave for a couple of minutes, then run a knife around the rim to loosen the cake from the tin and turn out on to a wire rack. Peel off the paper and leave until completely cold.

Lightly whip the cream until just thickened into soft peaks. If you have baked the cake in 1 tin, split in half horizontally with a serrated knife. Fill with jam and cream and sandwich together, so the cream forms the uppermost layer. If you have baked the cake in 2 tins, be sure to sandwich the flat bases together. Dust the top with icing sugar.

SERVES 8

FOR THE CAKE
175g unsalted butter, softened, plus more for the tin
175g self-raising flour
1 tsp baking powder
3 eggs, lightly beaten
175g golden caster sugar
1 tsp vanilla extract

FOR THE FILLING
150ml double cream
4 tbsp raspberry or strawberry jam
icing sugar, to dust

TO DECORATE see: Gala Cake, p92; Pink Iced Heart, p117; Fresh Petal Confetti Cake, p122; Butterfly Cakes, p153; Garland Cakes, p154; Rosebud Fairy Cakes, p157; Fondant Fancies, p163; Fancy Hats, p173

battenberg cake

This is serious retro territory! Reminiscent of our childhoods (when it came from a packet), it is said to have been created for the marriage of Queen Victoria's granddaughter to Prince Louis of Battenberg in 1884. Each square represents one of the 4 Battenberg princes: Louis, Alexander, Henry and Francis Joseph. It is exceptionally pretty and beats anything you can buy hands down.

Preheat the oven to 170°C/fan 160°C/340°F/gas mark 3½. Lightly butter a 20cm square tin and line the base with baking parchment. Also cut out a rectangle of baking parchment, as long and deep as the tin, to act as a divider lengthways between the 2 colours of sponge.

In the bowl of an electric mixer, or in a large bowl with a handheld whisk, first sift together the flour and baking powder. Add the butter, cut into knobs, the sugar, eggs and vanilla. Beat until smooth, adding a little milk to loosen the mixture if it seems too stiff. Weigh out half the batter and place the divider down the centre of the tin.

Carefully place half the batter into 1 side of the tin. Tint the remaining mixture pink - it's much better to do this not too exuberantly, so take care! - and stir until blended. As neatly as possible, spoon the pink mixture into the other side of the tin.

Bake for about 30–35 minutes, or until a skewer inserted into the centre comes out clean and the cake springs back to the touch. Remove from the oven, leave in the tin for a few minutes, then turn out on to a wire rack. When completely cold, slice each colour lengthways into 2 equal blocks, then trim off all the rough edges.

Warm the jam in a small pan, push it through a sieve, then use it to glue the strips of cake together lengthways, so the natural and pink colours form opposite quarters.

On a work surface dusted with icing sugar, roll out the marzipan into a rectangle the length of the cake and wide enough to wrap around all 4 sides. Trim it to size. Brush the remaining jam all over the cake and wrap the marzipan around the cake. Seal the join by gently pressing it together, then turn so this seam is hidden on the bottom. Trim the ends with a sharp knife, then score a criss-cross on the top surface.

SERVES 8

175g unsalted butter, softened, plus more for the tin
175g self-raising flour
½ tsp baking powder
175g white caster sugar
3 eggs, lightly beaten
1 tsp vanilla extract
1 or 2 tbsp milk, if needed
a little pink (or red) food colour
4 tbsp apricot jam
icing sugar, to dust
250g yellow marzipan (or natural if you prefer, see p138)

sticky ginger cake

A wonderful cake that should be left alone for a couple of days before eating... that's the hardest part! It's also delicious with my Salted Caramel Buttercream (see p64, use half the quantity).

Preheat the oven to 180°C/fan 170°C/350°F/gas mark 4. Butter a 20cm, 7.5cm deep, square tin and line with baking parchment.

Place the treacle, syrup, milk, sugar and butter into a pan and very gently melt together. Do not let this boil or it will curdle. Remove from the heat and cool a little.

In a large bowl, sift together the flour, ginger and bicarbonate of soda. Add the treacle mixture and fold together with a large spoon. Lastly, add the eggs, mix well and pour the batter into the tin. Knock a couple of times on a work surface to release any bubbles, then bake for 40-50 minutes until firm to the touch and a skewer inserted into the centre comes out clean.

Cool in the tin for about 15 minutes, then turn out on to a rack. When the cake is absolutely cold, wrap it in baking parchment and then in foil and leave for a couple of days. This will make it very moist with a slightly sticky surface.

When ready to serve, make the lime buttercream. Place the icing sugar and butter in the bowl of an electric mixer (or use a bowl and a handheld whisk) and beat for a good 5 minutes. Tip in the lime zest and slowly pour in the juice, still beating. Spread the buttercream over the cake. Scatter with the brandy snaps, if using.

SERVES 10

FOR THE CAKE
120g unsalted butter, plus more
    for the tin
125g black treacle
100g golden syrup
150ml milk
120g light muscovado sugar
225g plain flour
1 tbsp ground ginger
½ tsp bicarbonate of soda
2 eggs, lightly beaten
3 brandy snaps, lightly crushed
    (optional)

FOR THE LIME BUTTERCREAM
150g icing sugar, sifted
100g unsalted butter, softened
finely grated zest and juice of
    ½ large lime

TO DECORATE see: Mosaic Cake, p90

very lemony crunch cake

This moist sponge is doused in lemon syrup to give a wonderfully crunchy top.

Preheat the oven to 180°C/fan 170°C/350°F/gas mark 4.

Lightly butter an 18cm diameter, 7.5cm deep, round springform tin and line the base and sides with baking parchment.

Sift the flour and salt into a bowl and set aside. Melt the butter in a small pan and set aside to cool slightly. Using the whisk attachment of an electric mixer, or a bowl and electric whisk, beat the eggs and sugar together until very light and fluffy (this may take 5 minutes). Blend in the melted butter; then very gently fold in the flour and zest. Finally, slowly fold in the juice.

Pour the batter into the tin and bake for 30–35 minutes or until the cake springs back to the touch, or a skewer inserted into the centre comes out clean.

Meanwhile, make the crunchy topping by simply mixing the juice and sugar together in a small bowl. Immediately the cake comes from the oven, prick tiny holes all over it with a fine skewer or cocktail stick. Pour the lemon syrup evenly all over the surface. Leave to cool completely in the tin.

SERVES 6

FOR THE CAKE
175g unsalted butter, softened, plus more for the tin
175g self-raising flour
a pinch of salt
2 eggs, lightly beaten
175g golden caster sugar
zest, finely grated, and juice of 1 large unwaxed lemon

FOR THE TOPPING
juice of 1 large lemon
100g white granulated sugar

TO DECORATE see: Pansy Wreath, p104; Fairy Tale Garden Cakes, p178; Tiny Fairy Cakes, p181

orange drizzle cake

This is a very versatile recipe; try it with lemon zest and juice, too. It makes a firmer cake than the Very Lemony Crunch Cake (see p31), so is an excellent base for decorating.

Preheat the oven to 170°C/fan 160°C/340°F/gas mark 3 ½.

Butter a 20cm diameter, 7.5cm deep, round tin, then line the base with baking parchment.

Cream the butter, sugar and zest until very pale, light and fluffy (it will take at least 5 minutes in an electric mixer). Add the eggs gradually, beating between each addition, along with 1 tbsp of the flour to prevent curdling. Fold in the remaining flour and, lastly, slowly mix in the orange juice.

Pour the mixture into the prepared tin and bake for 40–45 minutes until the cake springs back to the touch, or a skewer inserted into centre comes out clean. Remove from the oven, leave for 1 minute, then turn out to cool on a wire rack.

Once the cake is absolutely cold, make the icing. Sift the icing sugar into a bowl and slowly add the orange juice and orange flower water, little by little, until the mixture coats the back of a spoon. Pour the icing over the cake, letting it drizzle down the sides.

SERVES 8

FOR THE CAKE
250g unsalted butter, softened, plus more for the tin
250g golden caster sugar
grated zest of 2 large oranges, plus 75ml orange juice
4 eggs, lightly beaten
250g self-raising flour, sifted

FOR THE ICING
200g icing sugar
juice of ½ orange
a few drops of orange flower water

TO DECORATE see: Maypole, p112; Tiered Marie Antoinette's Cake, p146; Crystallised Flower Fairy Cakes, p158; Ice-cream Cones, p160

genoese sponge

This classic French cake, the cornerstone of numerous gateaux, is very light. It is a little trickier than most of my other cakes, but provided the recipe is followed closely it should be as light as a feather. I have used no butter (except for the tin) so it does not keep well; eat it on the day it is made. If you like, try sprinkling a couple of spoonfuls of liqueur or syrup over the cake when it is cold. Use whatever you have, maybe Cointreau or cassis.

Preheat the oven to 180°C/170°C fan/350°F/gas mark 4. Butter a 23cm diameter, 7.5cm deep, round tin and line the base and sides with baking parchment.

Sift the flour and salt together into a bowl twice for extra fineness and lightness. Warm the whisk and bowl of an electric mixer by standing both in hot water, then drying thoroughly.

Crack the eggs into the bowl of the electric mixer, break them up a little with a fork, then add the sugar. Start the mixer slowly, then turn up the speed to its highest. You will see the mixture increasing in volume quite dramatically and becoming lighter and paler until it looks like a mousse. This may well take 5–6 minutes on full speed. It is crucial to stop at the right point, which is when you can drizzle a trail of mixture with the whisk which sits proud on the top of the rest of the batter for a few seconds; this is called the ribbon stage.

In 3 or 4 batches, fold in the flour as lightly as possible with a metal spoon, adding the vanilla as well. Inevitably, the mixture will start to lose the volume that you want to keep so, for the lightest result, do this as gently as you can.

Bake for 20–25 minutes, until the top springs back when lightly pressed with a finger and a skewer inserted into the centre comes out clean. Turn out on to a wire rack covered with a piece of baking parchment to stop the cake from sticking. Leave to cool completely.

Whip the cream until soft peaks form, adding the vanilla and the icing sugar, to taste. Slice the sponge in half horizontally, spread the cut side of each half with the cream and place all the fruits on top of one half. Sandwich together, then dust the top with icing sugar.

TO DECORATE see: Blackberry and Geranium Genoese, p87

SERVES 8

FOR THE CAKE
a little butter for the tin
125g plain flour
a pinch of salt
4 eggs
125g golden caster sugar
1 tsp vanilla extract

FOR THE FILLING
150ml double cream
1 tsp vanilla extract
2 tbsp icing sugar, or to taste, plus more to dust
250g fruit of your choice: sliced peaches or nectarines, strawberries, blueberries or raspberries

coffee and hazelnut cake

You can use filter, espresso or instant coffee... whatever you prefer and have in the cupboard. And you can choose which nuts you would like; you may want the more classic combination of coffee with walnut or pecan, or try almonds or even macadamias.

Preheat the oven to 180°C/fan 170°C/350°F/gas mark 4.

Lightly butter 2 x 20cm diameter, 4.5cm deep, sandwich tins, then line the bases with baking parchment.

Scatter the nuts for both the cake and the buttercream on to a baking sheet and roast in the oven for about 5 minutes, shaking once and watching carefully to make sure they don't burn, then remove from the oven and chop. Measure out and separate the amounts for both the cake and buttercream and set aside.

Sift together the flour and baking powder into a bowl and set aside. In an electric mixer, or in a large bowl with an electric whisk, cream together the butter and sugar for about 5 minutes until very light and fluffy. Add the eggs very slowly, with the mixer or whisk running, adding 1 tbsp of the flour during the process to prevent curdling. Finally, using a large spoon or spatula, fold in the remaining flour, the nuts, milk and coffee until well blended.

Divide the batter between the tins and bake for 25–30 minutes until the cakes spring back to the touch, or a skewer inserted into the centre comes out clean. Remove from the oven, leave them in their tins to cool slightly, then turn out on to a wire rack.

Meanwhile, make the buttercream. Cream the butter and sugar together for at least 5 minutes until really light and airy, then add the coffee. Mix well, then fold in some of the hazelnuts, keeping most back to decorate. Spread half the coffee buttercream on to the base of one cake, lay the other cake on top (flat bases together) and finish with the remaining buttercream. Scatter over the reserved hazelnuts.

TO DECORATE see: Giant Cupcake, p101

SERVES 8

FOR THE CAKE
225g unsalted butter, softened,
   plus more for the tin
60g hazelnuts, skinned
225g self-raising flour
1 tsp baking powder
225g light muscovado sugar
4 eggs, lightly beaten
2 tbsp milk
25ml very strong coffee

FOR THE BUTTERCREAM
60g hazelnuts, skinned
100g butter, softened
200g icing sugar
25ml very strong coffee

pistachio and orange blossom cake

I love the combination of delicate flavours here, and the creamy mascarpone topping acts as a perfect contrast.

Preheat the oven to 180°C/fan 170°C/350°F/gas mark 4. Lightly butter a 20cm diameter, 7.5cm deep, round loose-bottomed tin, and line with baking parchment.

Scatter the pistachios on to a baking sheet and roast in the oven for about 5 minutes, shaking once and watching all the time to make sure they don't burn. Allow to cool, then grind finely in a food processor.

In a large bowl, sift together the flour, baking powder and salt. Then, in an electric mixer, cream together the butter, sugar and zest until very light and fluffy - expect it to take about 5 minutes - and slowly add the eggs, adding 1 tbsp of the flour mixture as you do so to prevent curdling. Fold in the almonds and pistachios, the remaining flour and, lastly, the orange flower water.

Scrape the batter into the tin and bake for about 40 minutes, or until a skewer inserted into the centre comes out clean.

Meanwhile, make the syrup: tip the orange juice, sugar and orange flower water into a small pan and bring to a rolling boil. Cook until reduced to about 60ml.

Immediately the cake comes from the oven, prick it all over with a fine skewer or cocktail stick and evenly drizzle over the syrup. Leave to cool completely in the tin.

Turn the cake upside down on to a cake stand or plate, so the flat base now forms the top. Beat together all the ingredients for the mascarpone topping, and spread it on with a palette knife.

SERVES 8

FOR THE CAKE
175g unsalted butter, softened,
   plus more for the tin
100g shelled unsalted pistachios
70g self-raising flour
1 tsp baking powder
pinch of salt
200g golden caster sugar
zest of 1 orange, finely grated
4 eggs, lightly beaten
70g ground almonds
2 tsp orange flower water

FOR THE SYRUP
juice of 1 orange
45g golden caster sugar
1 tbsp orange flower water

FOR THE TOPPING
250g mascarpone
zest of 1 orange, finely grated
½ tsp vanilla extract
1 tsp orange flower water
30g golden caster sugar

TO DECORATE see: Rose Garden, p109

star anise, almond and clementine cake

The exotic flavour of star anise - a beautiful flower-shaped spice - permeates this lovely, moist cake. You can use lemongrass instead if you prefer for the syrup: split and slightly crush 2 stalks to bring out the flavour. You need to make the syrup a few hours in advance or, even better, the day before to allow the flavours to develop. Try this recipe with oranges if clementines are out of season.

A few hours before, or the day before, you start the cake, make the syrup. Gently boil together the clementine juice, sugar and star anise until it reduces to become a syrup, then cover and leave to infuse at room temperature to develop a good aniseed-orange flavour.

Preheat the oven to 180°C/fan 170°C/350°F/gas mark 4.

Butter a 20cm diameter, 7.5cm deep, round springform tin, then line the base and sides with baking parchment.

Cream the butter, sugar and zest together until very light and fluffy (this will take a good 5 minutes). Add the eggs very slowly then, with a large metal spoon, fold in the almonds, flour and baking powder.

Pour the batter into the cake tin, level the surface and bake for 45–50 minutes or until a skewer inserted into the centre comes out clean.

Immediately the cake is cooked, prick holes all over the surface with a fine skewer or cocktail stick and drizzle evenly with the syrup. Leave the star anise flowers from the syrup where they fall on the cake, for decoration. Allow to cool completely in the tin.

SERVES 8

FOR THE SYRUP
80ml clementine juice (about 2 fruits)
50g light muscovado sugar
5–6 star anise flowers

FOR THE CAKE
250g unsalted butter, softened, plus more for the tin
225g golden caster sugar
zest of 4 clementines, finely grated
4 eggs, lightly beaten
220g ground almonds
80g plain flour, sifted
1 tsp baking powder

TO DECORATE see: Eastern Fantasy, p89

carrot-pecan cake with maple syrup and orange buttercream

This moist cake rose to prominence in the 1970s and remains hugely popular. The flavours in the buttercream are a wonderful complement.

Preheat the oven to 160°C/fan 150°C/325°F/gas mark 3.

Oil a 23cm diameter, 7.5cm deep, round tin and line the base with baking parchment.

Scatter the pecans - both for cake and buttercream - on to a baking sheet and roast in the oven for about 5–10 minutes, shaking once and watching carefully so they don't burn, then measure out, separate and set aside the amounts needed for the cake and buttercream.

Sift together the flour, bicarbonate of soda, baking powder, salt, cinnamon and nutmeg into a large bowl. In an electric mixer - or in another large mixing bowl with a handheld electric whisk - slowly beat together the oil and sugar for a minute or so until smooth, then gradually add the eggs, beating well after each addition. Using a large spoon, gently fold in the carrot, zest, pecan nuts and coconut then, finally, the flour mixture.

Pour the batter into the tin and bake for 1 hour or until a skewer inserted into the centre comes out clean. Cool in the tin for a few minutes, then turn out on to a wire rack to become completely cold.

Meanwhile, make the buttercream. Beat the butter, icing sugar and maple syrup until really light and fluffy (this could take 5 minutes). In another bowl beat the cream cheese until smooth, then fold it into the butter mixture. Finally, add the orange juice. Spread over the top of the cake and scatter with the pecan nuts.

SERVES 10

FOR THE CAKE
175ml sunflower oil, plus more
  for the tin
60g pecan nuts, chopped
200g self-raising flour
½ tsp bicarbonate of soda
½ tsp baking powder
pinch of salt
2 tsp ground cinnamon
1 tsp nutmeg, freshly grated
175g light muscovado sugar
3 eggs, lightly beaten
250g carrot, finely grated
zest of 1 orange, finely grated
50g unsweetened desiccated
  coconut

FOR THE BUTTERCREAM
40g pecan nuts, chopped
80g unsalted butter
60g icing sugar, sifted
2 tbsp maple syrup
150g unsalted cream cheese
juice of 1 orange

TO DECORATE see: Daisy and Sunflower Cupcakes, p169;
  Mini Tiered Cakes, p175

tropical fruit cake

This gingery, rum-laced cake is a twist on the classic fruit cake. When I was dreaming this up, I thought of all the flavours of exotic sun-soaked holidays and put those in instead of the more usual fruits and nuts. You'll need to start this cake the day before to let the fruits soak up the rum.

The day before, rinse the cherries for the cake, then dry on kitchen towel and chop. Place the apricots, dates, ginger, sultanas, currants and cherries in a large bowl and pour over the rum, lime zest and juice. Give it all a good stir, cover with clingfilm and leave overnight.

Next day, preheat the oven to 140°C/fan 130°C/275°F/gas mark 1. Lightly butter a 20cm, 7.5 cm deep, square tin and line with baking parchment. Wrap the outside of the tin with a collar of brown paper (or even newspaper works fine) and tie with string. Do this every time you are baking fruit cakes that need long cooking, to protect the outsides from scorching in the tin.

Scatter the pistachios and pecans on to a baking tray and roast for 10 minutes. When cool, chop and set aside. Sift the flour, mixed spice, ground ginger and salt together. In the bowl of an electric mixer, cream together the butter and sugar until really light and fluffy (this will take at least 5 minutes). Add the ground almonds, then, very gradually, the eggs, mixing well after each addition. Add the flour mixture, the treacle and, lastly, gently fold in all the nuts and the fruits with their delicious rummy liquid.

Pour the mixture into the tin, levelling the top. Arrange the cherries, pecans and pistachios on top. Bake on a low oven shelf for about 2½-3 hours or until a skewer inserted into the centre comes out clean. If it browns too much before it is fully cooked, make a square of foil a bit larger than the cake, pierce a hole in the centre and open it up, then place it over the cake to protect the edges of the top surface.

Remove from the oven and leave to cool in the tin. When cold, prick all over with a fine skewer and sprinkle over the extra rum. Wrap in baking parchment, then foil, and leave to mature for a week - even a month - though it will still taste delicious if you need it straight away.

TO DECORATE see: Glacé Fruit and Nut Cake, p133; Christmas Gifts, p182

MAKES 25 SLICES

125g dark glacé cherries
150g ready-to-eat dried apricots, chopped
150g dates, chopped
200g glacé ginger, chopped
150g sultanas
150g currants
120ml dark rum (plus a couple of tbsp more to feed the cake)
finely grated zest and juice of 2 limes
295g unsalted butter, softened, plus more for the tin
100g shelled unsalted pistachios
100g pecan nuts
150g self-raising flour
1 tsp ground mixed spice
1 tbsp ground ginger
1 tsp salt
150g dark muscovado sugar
150g ground almonds
5 eggs, lightly beaten
2 tbsp black treacle

TO DECORATE
12 dark glacé cherries
18 pecans
24 shelled unsalted pistachios

rich tamarind fruit cake

I started my business using this particularly moist, dark recipe as a Christmas cake, producing hundreds of miniatures cooked in baked bean cans from my kitchen table (see p182 for more cakes cooked in cans). It has been tweaked by adding tamarind, my husband's bright idea! Make it up to 3 months in advance, or at least a week before you want it, to allow it to mature and absorb the brandy.

The day before, rinse the cherries, then dry them well with kitchen towel and cut each in half. Place the sultanas, raisins, currants, mixed peel, glacé ginger, cherries, tamarind paste, black treacle, marmalade, zests and mixed spice into a large bowl. Pour over the brandy, give it a stir, cover with clingfilm and leave overnight.

Next day, preheat the oven to 140ºC/fan 130ºC/275ºF/gas mark 1. Lightly butter a 23cm diameter, 7.5cm deep, round tin and line with baking parchment. Wrap the outside of the tin with brown paper and tie with string, to protect the edges from scorching in the oven.

Scatter the whole nuts on a baking sheet and roast for 10 minutes in the oven, shaking once and watching so they don't burn. Cool slightly, chop and set aside.

Sift the flour and salt into a bowl. In an electric mixer, beat the butter and sugar for at least 5 minutes until paler and fluffy. Add the ground almonds, then very gradually the eggs, mixing well between each addition. Fold in the flour with a large metal spoon and, lastly, all the fruits (and any liquid) and nuts.

Scrape the batter into the tin and bake on a low shelf for about 2¾–3 hours. Start to check it after 2½ hours: if a skewer inserted into the centre comes out clean, it is ready. If it browns too much before it is fully cooked, make a circle of foil a bit larger than the cake, pierce a hole in the centre and open it up, then place it over the tin.

Remove from the oven and cool in the tin. When cold, prick all over with a fine skewer and evenly sprinkle over the extra brandy. Wrap in baking parchment, then foil, and leave to mature for a week or up to 3 months. Unwrap and feed it with 1 tbsp more brandy every other week, if you like, for extra succulence and booziness!

TO DECORATE see: Christmas Trees, p130; Gingerbread Man Cake, p137; Vintage Glamour Wedding Cake, p140

MAKES 25–30 SLICES

200g dark glacé cherries
280g sultanas
280g raisins, preferably lexia or muscatel
100g currants
170g mixed peel
110g glacé ginger, chopped
1 tsp tamarind paste
3 tbsp black treacle
40g bitter marmalade
zest of 1 unwaxed lemon, finely grated
zest of 1 orange, finely grated
1 heaped tbsp mixed spice
100ml brandy, plus 3 tbsp to feed the cake
250g unsalted butter, softened, plus more for the tin
120g walnuts
40g blanched almonds
180g self-raising flour
1 tsp salt
250g dark muscovado sugar
160g ground almonds
5 eggs, lightly beaten

whisky, date and walnut cake

Whisky and shortbread may be Scotland's greatest culinary exports and, due to my Scottish roots, both have found their way into this book. If you can sneak in a splash of malt whisky it will make it extra special. You'll need to start the cake the day before, to plump up the fruits in whisky.

The day before, place the cherries and dates in a bowl and pour on the whisky. Mix well, cover with clingfilm and leave overnight.

Preheat the oven to 140°C/fan 130°C/275°F/gas mark 1. Butter a large (30x11x6.5cm) loaf tin, or a 20cm diameter, 7.5cm deep, round tin, or a 20cm square tin, and line with baking parchment. Wrap the tin with a collar of brown paper tied with string.

Roast the walnuts on a baking sheet in the oven for 10 minutes - watching so they don't burn - then roughly chop. Using an electric mixer, or a large bowl and wooden spoon, cream together the butter, sugar and zests for a good 5 minutes until light and fluffy. Next, add the ground almonds, then gradually beat in the eggs, mixing thoroughly between each addition. Add the treacle, then fold in the flour. Finally, very gently fold in the nuts, cherries and dates, along with any whisky that has not been absorbed. Add enough milk to give the mixture a dropping consistency.

Pour the batter into the tin, level with a palette knife, decorate with the remaining walnuts and place in the oven. Bake for about 1½ hours, or until a skewer inserted into the centre comes out clean.

Remove from the oven and leave the cake to cool in the tin. When completely cold, prick with a fine skewer and drizzle in the extra whisky. Wrap the cake in baking parchment, then in foil, and store for up to a month.

MAKES 12 SLICES

100g glacé cherries, halved
140g dates, stoned and quartered
90ml whisky (plus a couple of tbsp more to feed the cake)
150g unsalted butter, softened, plus more for the tin
250g walnuts, plus 5 more half-walnuts for decoration
150g dark muscovado sugar
zest of 1 orange, finely grated
zest of 1 unwaxed lemon, finely grated
2 tbsp ground almonds
3 eggs, lightly beaten
1 tbsp black treacle
225g self-raising flour, sifted
40ml milk

TO DECORATE see: Marzipan Criss-Cross, p138

cherry and marzipan cake

Use the best cherries you can find. If you can get glacé sour cherries (I used some from Poland), then do try them - they elevate this recipe into something very special - though it does still taste great with normal glacé cherries. The layer of marzipan melts into the sponge.

Preheat the oven to 170ºC/fan 160ºC/340ºF/gas mark 3 ½. Butter a 30x11x6.5cm loaf tin, or a 23cm round cake tin, and line the base with baking parchment.

Rinse and completely dry the cherries on kitchen towel. Sift the flour and baking powder into a bowl and set aside. Roll out the marzipan between 2 sheets of clingfilm into a very thin rectangle or circle, slightly smaller than the tin, and set aside.

Cream the butter, sugar and zest together in an electric mixer until very pale, light and fluffy (this will take about 5 minutes).

Beat in the eggs a little at a time, adding 1 tbsp flour during the process to stop the mixture from curdling. Fold in the almonds, the sifted flour mixture and the lemon juice until well blended, then spoon half the cake mixture into the tin. Place half the cherries over the batter in a shape echoing that of the tin, towards the middle. This will support the marzipan. Lay on the marzipan, then add the remaining cherries, again in a shape echoing the tin, but this time towards the outer edge. Pour in the remaining batter. Sprinkle over the demerara and bake for 50-60 minutes. It's ready when a skewer comes out clean and the centre of the cake springs back to the touch.

Cool the cake in the tin for 15-20 minutes, then turn out and remove the paper. Leave to cool completely. Don't worry if it sinks a bit in the middle; it's due to the weight of the marzipan and cherries. If decorating, simply invert it so the flat base forms the top.

SERVES 8

225g unsalted butter, softened, plus more for the tin
200g whole undyed glacé cherries
225g self-raising flour
½ tsp baking powder
120g marzipan (see p138)
225g golden caster sugar
zest of 1 unwaxed lemon, finely grated, plus 2 tbsp lemon juice
4 eggs, lightly beaten
115g ground almonds
2 tbsp demerara sugar

TO DECORATE see: Summer Cherries, p95; Ribbon Roses, p120; Fluttering Butterflies, p125

vegan fruit cake

For all the vegans, those with allergies to dairy products or indeed anyone wanting a speedy, delicious fruit cake, this is for you. It contains neither eggs nor butter, has very little added sugar, is packed with moist fruit and roasted nuts, then laced with rum. The recipe was originally devised for Sir Paul McCartney at Christmas.

Preheat the oven to 140ºC/fan 130ºC/275ºF/gas mark 1.

Oil a 23cm diameter, 7.5cm deep, round tin, and line with baking parchment. Wrap the outside of the tin with brown paper and tie it securely with string.

Chop all the nuts and roast in the oven for 10–15 minutes, watching carefully to make sure they don't burn. Place the dried fruits, oil, orange juice and sugar in a heavy-based pan, add 300ml water, then bring to the boil and simmer over a gentle heat for 5 minutes. Cool, then fold in all the other ingredients. Transfer the batter to the prepared tin and bake for 2 ½ hours, or until a skewer inserted into the middle comes out clean. If it browns too much before it is fully cooked, make a circle of foil a bit larger than the cake, break a large hole in the centre and place it over the cake to protect the sides.

Allow to cool in the tin, turn out on to a wire rack, prick all over with a fine skewer and sprinkle the remaining rum all over the cake.

Wrap in baking parchment, then in foil, and store for up to 6 weeks.

SERVES 15 SLICES

150ml sunflower oil, plus more for the tin
50g blanched almonds
50g walnuts
300g raisins (lexia or muscatel, if possible)
250g sultanas
125g currants
150ml orange juice
75g light muscovado sugar
350g self-raising flour, sifted
1 tbsp black treacle
zest of 1 unwaxed lemon, finely grated
zest of 1 orange, finely grated
¼ tsp salt
1 tsp mixed spice
3 tbsp rum or brandy, plus 3 tbsp more to feed the cake

TO DECORATE see: Fruit Cake Fairy Cakes, p186

exotic fruit chewy meringue

A crisp meringue with a soft marshmallowy centre, lavishly topped with a tangy lemon and passion fruit cream and winter fruits. Here we photographed just a 25cm single disc, which would need exactly half the ingredients given and serve 6. If you want to make this smaller meringue, be generous with the fruits and use about 600g. Do read my tips on perfect meringues (see p71) before you begin.

Line 2 baking sheets with baking parchment. Preheat the oven to 210°C/fan 200°C/410°F/gas mark 7. Draw 3 circles on baking parchment, the first 10cm in diameter, another 18cm and the last 25cm (use plates, saucers or cans as a guide).

Stir together the cornflour and vinegar in a small bowl until well blended. In a large, clean bowl, whisk the egg whites and salt with a handheld whisk, or in an electric mixer, until they hold their shape in soft peaks. Add the sugar 1 tbsp at a time, alternating with a little of the cornflour. The meringue should be thick, shiny and marshmallowy.

Using a spatula, spread the mixture into the 3 drawn circles. Keep the discs reasonably flat. Put them in the oven and immediately reduce the temperature to very, very low (mine was at 80°C/fan 70°C/175°F/gas mark ¼). Bake for 1¾–2 hours. They should be crispy and dry on the outside and may be a bit cracked, which is fine. Give them a bit longer in the oven if necessary, but they may start to colour a little; try to keep them as white as possible. Turn the oven off, leave the door slightly ajar and allow them to cool completely in the oven.

Whip the cream until soft peaks form, then fold in the vanilla and sugar to taste. Half fold in the lemon curd. Cut open the passion fruit and scoop out the seeds. Peel and stone the mango and chop. Peel the pineapple and chop into bite-sized pieces. Deseed the pomegranate. Place the largest meringue on a serving plate. Spread with some cream, then a layer of fruit, reserving a few pomegranate seeds. Add more cream, then place on the 18cm meringue. Repeat with the remaining cream and fruits and top with the smallest meringue. Sprinkle with the reserved pomegranate, dust liberally with icing sugar and a little edible glitter, if you wish.

TO DECORATE see: Summer Berry Rose-scented Meringue, p114

SERVES 12

FOR THE MERINGUE
4 tsp cornflour
4 tsp white wine vinegar
8 egg whites
pinch of salt
400g white caster sugar

FOR THE FILLING
600ml double cream
2 tsp vanilla extract or seeds from 1 vanilla pod
4 tbsp icing sugar, plus more to dust
6 tbsp lemon curd
3 ripe, crinkly passion fruit
800g mixed exotic fruits of your choice, I used mangoes, pineapple and pomegranate
1 pot clear edible glitter (optional)

surprise fridge cake

This recipe has 2 huge advantages: not only will you become unbelievably popular overnight with your children (it disappeared, mysteriously, very quickly in our household), it's also a doddle. The surprise is that, hidden inside, are your children's favourite sweets. Of course, you could always make it healthier by using chopped dried fruits and nuts instead, but you might not be so popular!

You will need a 24x11cm loaf tin or terrine, or the equivalent square tin. Butter the tin and line it with clingfilm, allowing a generous excess to overhang the edges.

Crush the biscuits into small pieces by placing them in a polythene bag and bashing with a rolling pin. In a small pan, very gently melt together the butter, sugar, syrup, cocoa and chocolate. Remove from the heat and cool until tepid. Add the biscuits and stir in the chocolates and sweets. Mix well and spoon into the tin. Cover the top with the excess clingfilm and set in the refrigerator for a few hours. Once set, remove the cake from the tin by pulling on the clingfilm and easing it out with a knife. Turn it out on to a serving plate.

For the topping, place a small heatproof bowl over a saucepan of gently simmering water, making sure the base of the bowl does not touch the water. Add the chocolate to the bowl and heat until it melts, stirring only very occasionally, then pour over the cake. Store in the refrigerator - preferably hidden! - until you serve it. It will cut much more easily if it is not kept for too long at room temperature.

SERVES 12

FOR THE CAKE
110g unsalted butter, cubed, plus more for the tin
150g plain biscuits
90g golden caster sugar
2 tbsp golden syrup
1 tbsp cocoa
50g 50% cocoa solids chocolate, broken into pieces
150g chocolates and sweets (I used mini marshmallows, crushed honeycomb chocolate bars, malted chocolate balls and caramel chocolates)

FOR THE TOPPING
75–100g 50% cocoa solids chocolate, broken into pieces

TO DECORATE see: Penguin Cake, p134; Melting Snowmen, p185

dark chocolate mousse cake

A surprisingly light chocolate mousse on a base of
Chocolate Tiffin (see p68). This is really simple, but
the trick is that both the cream and chocolate need to
be at room temperature. Keep the cake in the refrigerator
until shortly before serving.

Butter a round 23cm springform tin, ensuring the rim is facing down
so it is easy to remove the cake later. Fill the base with the Chocolate
Tiffin, levelling it evenly by pressing with the back of a teaspoon, and
leave it to set for a few hours in the refrigerator.

Melt the chocolate in a good-sized bowl set over a pan of barely
simmering water (make sure the base of the bowl does not touch the
water), then add the kirsch. Cool until the mixture is just at blood
temperature. In a large bowl, whisk the cream until slightly thickened
and the whisk leaves a trail.

Now, very gently whisk half the cream into the chocolate, then fold
in the remaining cream, until thoroughly blended and smooth. Be
gentle. Pour into the tin and chill overnight in the refrigerator.

When ready to serve, remove from the refrigerator and dip a knife
into hot water before running it all around the edge, then lift on to
a serving plate or cake stand. You should be able to loosen the tiffin
from the base of the tin by running a palette knife between them.
Finish with a dusting of cocoa powder, if you wish. This cake can't be
left a long time at room temperature, so serve shortly after it comes
out of the refrigerator.

SERVES 12

butter, for the tin
1 x recipe Chocolate Tiffin
    (see p68)
300g 50–70% cocoa solids
    chocolate, broken into pieces
1 tbsp kirsch or Cointreau
500ml whipping cream
1 tbsp cocoa powder, to dust
    (optional)

TO DECORATE see: Easter Chocolate Truffle Cake, p111

caramelised vanilla millefeuille

This is a very simple, quick cake – using just a few storecupboard ingredients – and produces layers of caramelised flaky puff pastry leaves scattered with roasted nuts and sandwiched with a vanilla toffee cream. Dulce de leche is a wonderful caramel sauce from Argentina; find it in most good supermarkets.

Preheat the oven to 200ºC/fan 190ºC/400ºF/gas mark 6.

Scatter the nuts on to a baking sheet and roast for 4–5 minutes (it won't take long as the oven is hot). Watch carefully so they don't burn. Cool, then chop. Line 2 or 3 baking sheets with baking parchment.

Roll out the pastry on a surface well dusted with icing sugar to a thickness of about 4mm. You need a large rectangle from which you will cut 3 equal-sized smaller rectangles. Prick each pastry about 6 times with a fork and rest in the refrigerator for about 30 minutes.

Alternatively, if you want a circular cake, cut out 2 x 20cm circles, using cake tins or plates as guides. Take the pastry offcuts, roll them out again and cut a third circle. Place all 3 on the baking sheets, prick with a fork and rest in the refrigerator for about 30 minutes.

When ready to bake, remove the pastry from the refrigerator, sprinkle over the icing sugar and bake until the sugar is melted and bubbling and the pastry is a lovely golden brown; this can take from 12 to 20 minutes. Watch carefully, as a few minutes too long and the pastry will burn. Remove from the oven and allow to cool on the sheets for a minute or 2, then peel off the parchment and cool on wire racks. These may be cooked a few hours in advance, though be sure only to add the filling an hour or 2 before serving.

Whip the cream to soft peaks and stir in 2 tbsp dulce de leche and the vanilla. Place a pastry on to a cake stand or serving plate. Sandwich all 3 layers together, spreading the bottom and the middle layers with dulce de leche, then a layer of toffee cream (piped on or spread with a knife) and a sprinkling of nuts. Finish by placing the top layer on the cake with a final dusting of icing sugar and a last sprinkling of nuts. To serve, cut with a very sharp knife in a gentle sawing action.

SERVES 8

100g pistachios, hazelnuts or pecan nuts, skinned
375g bought all-butter puff pastry
2 tbsp icing sugar, plus more to dust
300ml double cream
300g dulce de leche
seeds from 1 vanilla pod, or 1 tsp vanilla extract
1 large star nozzle (optional)
1 nylon piping bag (optional)

strawberry, mint and balsamic cheesecake

I find many cheesecakes too dense, but not this exceptionally light, summery version. The balsamic vinegar enhances the flavour of the strawberries wonderfully.

Preheat the oven to 170ºC/fan 160ºC/340ºF/gas mark 3½. Butter very well the base and sides of a 23cm diameter, 7.5cm deep, round springform tin, making sure the flat side of the springform base is uppermost (the lipped side makes it hard to remove the cheesecake).

Put the biscuits in a polythene bag, seal, then bash with a rolling pin until very fine. Tip into a bowl and mix in the butter and mint. Lightly press into the tin with a spoon. Bake for 15 minutes, then leave to cool.

For the strawberry filling, simply mix everything together in a bowl and leave for 1–2 hours for the strawberries to absorb the flavours. Drain the strawberries, reserving all the delicious juices.

For the cream cheese filling, place 3 tbsp cold water into a small, wide-bottomed heatproof bowl and sprinkle over the gelatine. Every single crystal must be wet, or it will turn to lumps later on. Set the bowl over a pan of hot (not boiling) water until every crystal has melted. Don't let it get too hot or it won't set properly.

In a small bowl, beat the cream cheese until smooth. In another bowl, lightly whip the cream and vanilla. Using an electric mixer (or handheld whisk), whisk the egg yolks and sugar until thick, pale and doubled in volume. Carefully fold in the cream cheese, then the cream. Take the strawberry juices and mix them into the gelatine liquid, sieve out any lumps, then fold in a spoonful of the cream mixture. Once well blended, gently fold in the remaining cream.

Spread the marinated strawberries over the centre of the biscuit base, ensuring they do not reach the edges. Spoon on the cream, level the surface and place in the refrigerator overnight to set.

When you are ready to serve, dip a knife into hot water, release the spring and run the knife around the edge of the tin. Ease off the base with a warm palette knife and transfer to a serving dish. Finally, decorate with the sliced strawberries and mint sprigs.

SERVES 10–12

FOR THE BASE
50g unsalted butter, melted, plus more for the tin
300g dark chocolate digestive biscuits
10 large mint leaves, finely chopped

FOR THE STRAWBERRY FILLING
300g strawberries, thinly sliced
1 tsp balsamic vinegar
10 large mint leaves, finely chopped
1 tbsp icing sugar

FOR THE CREAM CHEESE FILLING
3 tsp gelatine crystals
250g unsalted cream cheese, at room temperature
300ml double cream
1 tsp vanilla extract
3 large egg yolks
45g golden caster sugar

TO DECORATE
150–200g strawberries
few sprigs of mint

sticky toffee cupcakes
with salted caramel buttercream

Everybody's favourite pudding brought bang up-to-date as a cupcake with salted caramel buttercream. There are 2 alternative toppings: the first involves making a caramel; the second, simply opening a jar of dulce de leche. The choice is yours, though the former will give a pleasing bitter edge. If you prefer an unsalted caramel buttercream, omit the salt and use unsalted butter.

Preheat the oven to 180ºC/fan 170ºC/350ºF/gas mark 4. Place the paper cases into a cupcake tin. In a heatproof bowl, pour 180ml boiling water over the dates and leave to soak for 20 minutes. Then, with a fork, gently break up the dates and stir in the vanilla.

Sift the flour and bicarbonate of soda into a bowl and set aside. Cream together the butter and sugar for a good 5 minutes until very light and fluffy. Add the eggs gradually, beating between each addition and slipping in 1 tbsp flour about halfway through to prevent curdling. Lastly, fold in the remaining flour and then the date mixture. Spoon into the cupcake cases and bake for 15–20 minutes (the tops should spring back when pressed with a finger). Remove and leave to cool.

Meanwhile, make the buttercream. To make the caramel, dissolve the sugar and 60ml water in a small, solid-based pan over a gentle heat, then increase the heat to a boil. Wait a few minutes, leaving the pan undisturbed but watching it like a hawk and, as soon as it changes to a wonderful caramel colour (like strong tea) and is thicker, remove immediately from the heat, stand well back, and add the cream. Be very careful as it is searing hot and it may splatter a little. It will react, or 'seize', and you may think it has gone wrong; it hasn't. Keep stirring, adding the salt and the vanilla. Leave until stone cold.

If using dulce de leche, simply mix it with the salt and vanilla.

Cream the butter and icing sugar for at least 5 minutes in an electric mixer (or use a handheld mixer) and add the caramel or the dulce de leche. Put the buttercream into the piping bag fitted with the star nozzle and pipe it on to the cakes, or spread it on with a palette knife.

MAKES 12

FOR THE CAKES
12 cupcake cases
180g dates, pitted and chopped
1 tsp vanilla extract
180g self-raising flour
1 tsp bicarbonate of soda
80g unsalted butter, softened
150g light muscovado sugar
2 eggs, lightly beaten

FOR THE BUTTERCREAM
1 CARAMEL METHOD
125g white caster sugar
80ml double cream
½ tsp salt (or to taste)
1 tsp vanilla extract

2 DULCE DE LECHE METHOD
3–4 tbsp dulce de leche
½ tsp salt (or to taste)
1 tsp vanilla extract

160g salted butter, softened
200g icing sugar, sifted
nylon piping bag (optional)
medium or large star nozzle
 (optional)

TO DECORATE see: Flying Insects, p176

floral macaroons

These glamorous creations have become highly fashionable and it's easy to see why. I've given 4 colours and flavours here – rose, lavender, orange and pistachio - though as you improve, you could experiment with the whole rainbow of colours and flavours. This is a tricky recipe, but do try it; if you follow the instructions carefully and read my perfect meringue tips (p71) it is very satisfying. The macaroons can be made ahead and freeze very well without their filling.

Line 2 baking sheets with baking parchment.

Sift the icing sugar into a bowl and stir in the almonds. In an electric mixer, whisk the egg whites with a few drops of the chosen food colour, starting slowly then increasing the speed, until soft peaks form. Slowly add the caster sugar and vanilla and whisk for about another minute until firm. Gently fold in half of the ground almond mixture, then the other half, until smooth.

Preheat the oven to 160ºC/fan 150ºC/325ºF/gas mark 3. Spoon the mixture into the piping bag and pipe 2cm rounds on to the trays, spacing them 3cm or so apart. If there are any peaks, they are easily removed by very slightly moistening your finger with water and pressing down gently on to the peak. Set aside for about 30 minutes; they should have slightly skinned over. Bake in the oven for 10–15 minutes with the door wedged slightly open (I use a wooden spoon handle). The macaroons are ready when you can lift them off the baking parchment. Remove from the oven and cool on a wire rack. (If any stick to the baking parchment, rub a slightly damp cloth on the underside of the paper and they should detach.)

To make the rose, orange flower or pistachio fillings, place the chocolate into a bowl. Bring the cream to the boil in a small pan and pour it over the chocolate. Leave for 1–2 minutes, then lightly stir together until smooth, adding your chosen flavourings.

For the lavender filling, bring the lavender and cream to just below the boil, then leave aside for 30 minutes to infuse. Strain out the lavender, then bring the cream to the boil once more and proceed as above with the white chocolate.

Chill the fillings slightly, then whisk until thickened and fill the macaroons. They will keep in the fridge for a couple of days.

MAKES ABOUT 80 MACAROONS, 40 WHEN SANDWICHED TOGETHER

200g icing sugar
120g ground almonds
3 egg whites, at room
    temperature
a few drops of food colour: pink,
    purple, orange or green
20g white caster sugar
½ tsp vanilla extract
nylon piping bag with 1cm nozzle

FOR THE FILLING
100g Swiss white chocolate,
    finely chopped
100ml double cream

ROSE
1 tsp rosewater

ORANGE FLOWER
zest of 1 orange, finely grated
1 tsp orange flower water

PISTACHIO
1 tbsp ground unsalted pistachios

LAVENDER
6 lavender heads

gilded chocolate tiffin

Fruit and nut chocolate bars will never taste the same again after you try these! A cross between a delicious chocolate and a good biscuit, they can be served any time, but seem especially appropriate after dinner. The gold leaf adds luxury. I always make them at Christmas and they can be a very special gift, packed into a beautiful box. If you want to make nuggets, you will need silicone petit four tins.

Lightly butter a 20cm square tin or Swiss roll tin and line it with clingfilm; this will make it easier to remove the tiffin later.

Preheat the oven to 170ºC/fan 160ºC/340ºF/gas mark 3 ½. Scatter the nuts on to a baking sheet and roast in the oven for about 5 minutes, shaking once and watching carefully to make sure they don't burn, then remove and chop into chunks.

Find a bowl that will fit over a pan of simmering water, making sure the base of the bowl does not touch the water. In the bowl, melt the butter, syrup and chocolate together. Place the biscuits in a large polythene bag, seal the top, then bash with a rolling pin until very finely crushed. Add the nuts, dried fruit and biscuits to the butter mixture and stir until all is very well blended.

Spoon into the prepared tin (or the silicone moulds, if you are making nuggets) and set in the refrigerator for at least 4 hours. If you have used a tin, wait until the tiffin is set, then bring to room temperature to make it easier to cut (it might crack if too chilled). Cut into 3cm squares, wiping the knife with kitchen towel between slices.

The gold leaf needs to be applied very carefully in a room with no draughts. Take 1 square of tiffin or nugget at a time on to a work surface. Place the gold booklet close by and slide off 1 sheet, by gently holding the top 2 corners with the tips of the 2 paint brushes, using both hands. Static will cause the bristles to grip the sheet. Try not to breathe on or touch the gold before it is on the tiffin!

Loosely place the gold on a tiffin square, or wrap it around a nugget, then smooth it down with a paint brush. If it tears, it doesn't matter, you can choose to patch it or leave it as it is with the chocolate showing through. You can either lay the gold randomly over the squares, leaving many of them plain, or wrap each nugget completely in gold. Store in the refrigerator... or maybe the safe!

MAKES 36 SQUARES OR 27
GOLDEN NUGGETS

FOR THE TIFFIN
100g unsalted butter, diced, plus
   more for the tin
80g shelled, unsalted pistachios
   (or hazelnuts or pine nuts)
1 tbsp golden syrup
100g 70% cocoa solids
   chocolate, broken into pieces
100g plain biscuits (or even
   unsweetened cornflakes)
80g dried sour cherries (or
   dried blueberries, cranberries,
   apricots or figs), finely chopped

TO GILD
4–20 sheets of loose gold leaf, to
   taste and to budget!
2 small paint brushes

tiny meringues

These dinky little meringues remind me of those my mother made. At any family celebration they were piled high, clouds of crispy white billows, oozing with cream, dusted with cocoa and finished with a crystallised violet. To me they were the most sublime dessert in the world.

Preheat the oven to 140°C/fan 130°C/275°F/gas mark 1 and line 2 baking sheets with baking parchment.

Place the egg whites and salt in the bowl of an electric mixer, or use a handheld whisk and a large ceramic bowl. Whisk on a low speed, then increase the speed until the egg whites form stiff peaks. Add the caster sugar 1 tbsp at a time, whisking between each addition. It should become stiff and glossy after 4–5 minutes. Do not over-mix. Sift over half the icing sugar and very gently fold in with a large metal spoon, then fold in the remainder. Again, be careful not to over-mix.

Now either use the piping bag and nozzle to pipe 4cm diameter meringues on to the baking sheets, or make quenelles (little ovals) by shaping the mixture between 2 teaspoons. Bake for 25–35 minutes. They are cooked when the underside sounds hollow when tapped. Carefully remove from the paper and cool on a wire rack.

Whip the cream lightly with the vanilla and spread it over the bases of half the meringues, then sandwich with the others. Arrange on a serving plate, dust with cocoa and top each with a crystallised violet.

MAKES 50 MINI MERINGUES, OR
25 MERINGUE SANDWICHES

3 egg whites, at room
    temperature
pinch of salt
85g white caster sugar
85g icing sugar
large nylon piping bag (optional)
medium star nozzle (optional)
150ml double cream
1 tsp vanilla extract
cocoa powder, to dust
25–30 crystallised violets

perfect meringues

Egg whites hate grease, so be punctilious about cleaning the bowl. Use metal, glass or ceramic, as plastic bowls are harder to degrease. Wipe the bowl with a cut lemon, then dry thoroughly before using. Egg whites don't like water, not even a drop.

Use good-quality eggs at room temperature; slightly older eggs give most volume. Beat with an electric whisk; it's hard work otherwise! Line baking sheets with baking parchment, not greaseproof as the meringues will stick. Dab a little meringue on the underside of the parchment to glue it to the baking sheet.

gingerbread biscuits

Once you have wrapped the dough in clingfilm to chill, you can store it in the refrigerator for a couple of days or freeze for up to a month so they are ready to bake at any time.

Sift the flour, spices and bicarbonate of soda into a large bowl and add the butter, cut into small chunks. Gently rub together with your fingertips - or pulse in a food processor - until the mixture resembles fine breadcrumbs

Add the egg yolk, sugar, syrup, treacle and zest and mix together until you have a firm dough. If it's too sticky, mix in a little more flour. Wrap in clingfilm and chill for at least 1 hour. Preheat the oven to 180°C/fan 170°C/350°F/gas mark 4. Line 2 baking sheets with baking parchment. Roll out the dough on a lightly floured surface to 4mm thick, and cut out with a 6.5cm round cutter. Bake for 10–15 minutes. The gingerbreads will have darkened a little.

Remove from the oven and leave to firm up a little for a few minutes, then gently transfer to a wire rack to cool. They will become crisp.

MAKES ABOUT 40

350g plain flour, plus more
   to dust
4 tsp ground ginger
1 tsp ground cinnamon
½ tsp bicarbonate of soda
130g salted butter, very
   slightly softened
1 egg yolk
150g light muscovado sugar
3 tbsp golden syrup
2 tbsp black treacle
zest of 1 orange, finely grated

TO DECORATE see: Autumn Leaves, p196; Stained Glass Tree Decorations, p199; Gingerbread Mobile, p201

classic shortbread

My Scottish grandmother always baked shortbread with rice flour, but you can choose cornflour if you prefer: rice flour will give a granulated, crunchy result, while cornflour produces biscuits that melt in the mouth. I always have a batch of these stored raw in the freezer so, at very short notice, I can fill the house with the gorgeous scent of freshly baked shortbread. Beats opening a packet. Use a selection of cutters; my favourites are hearts, stars or simple rounds.

Preheat the oven to 170°C/fan 160°C/340°F/gas mark 3½. Using a large bowl and a wooden spoon, or a handheld electric whisk, or an electric mixer, cream together the butter and sugar, then sift in the flour and cornflour gradually, mixing briefly between each addition, until it binds together. Flour your hands and gently knead until just smooth (do not over-work). To make the dough easier to roll – and if you have time – wrap in clingfilm and refrigerate for 30 minutes.

On a floured board, roll out the dough to 5–6mm thick, then cut into your chosen shapes. I used a 4.5cm heart-shaped cutter. If the shortbread is to be frozen, lay the biscuits between sheets of baking parchment in a freezer container. They need to be defrosted for 1 hour before baking. Place the shortbreads on 2 baking sheets lined with baking parchment and cook for 15–20 minutes. Sprinkle with sugar, then cool for 10 minutes before carefully transferring to a wire rack.

flavourings
Add any of these to the butter and sugar before adding the flour:

vanilla seeds of 1 vanilla pod and ½ tsp vanilla extract

orange-cardamom zest of 1 orange, finely grated, and ½ tsp freshly ground cardamom seeds, sifted

lemon-lavender zest of 1 unwaxed lemon, finely grated, and 4 tsp fresh lavender flowers

cinnamon 2 tsp ground cinnamon

coffee 1 tbsp instant or filter coffee dissolved in 1 tsp boiling water

salt and pepper 24 turns of a pepper mill, or to taste; also sprinkle more pepper on top with the caster sugar

TO DECORATE see: Iced, Layered Shortbread, p190

MAKES ABOUT 60

500g salted butter, softened
200g golden caster sugar, plus more to sprinkle
500g plain flour, plus more to dust
250g cornflour or rice flour

vanilla butter biscuits

This is a very useful recipe as it is so versatile; it can be rolled quite thinly and holds its shape very well once baked. I used a 7.5cm blossom cutter, but make any shape you prefer.

Sift the flour and salt into a bowl and set aside. Cream together the butter and sugar in a large bowl, using a wooden spoon - or in a food mixer - until well combined and fluffy. Add the egg yolk and vanilla and mix it in well, then work in the flour. Once the mixture comes together as a dough, dust your hands with flour and wrap it in clingfilm. Chill for an hour (or up to a few days if more convenient) or freeze for up to a month. This dough can otherwise be tricky to work, especially in hot weather or a warm kitchen. When ready to bake, preheat the oven to 180ºC/fan 170ºC/350ºF/gas mark 4.

Roll out the dough on a floured board to 3mm thick, using plenty of flour as it is quite sticky. (You could even roll it between 2 sheets of clingfilm if that makes it easier.) Cut out into your preferred shapes and place on 2 baking sheets lined with baking parchment. Bake for 12–15 minutes until pale gold. Remove from the oven and leave to cool on the trays for a few minutes before carefully transferring to a wire rack. They will firm up as they cool. Leave until completely cold.

Put the chocolate into a bowl over gently simmering water, ensuring the base of the bowl does not touch the water. Stir occasionally until melted. Cool slightly, then spoon into the piping bag. Seal the bag and snip the end. Drizzle the chocolate over the biscuits to decorate.

MAKES 40

370g plain flour, plus more to dust
½ tsp salt
250g unsalted butter, diced
125g golden caster sugar
1 egg yolk
1 tsp vanilla extract
100g dark or milk chocolate, broken into pieces
1 large piping bag or freezer bag

TO DECORATE see: Doily Biscuits, p192; Easter Tree Decorations, p195

decorate

big cakes

23-carat gold cake

Real opulence on a plate: a dark, rich, luxurious chocolate cake encased in pure gold. Gold has been used to decorate food for centuries and has no taste or smell. This is a showstopper - a real centrepiece for an important occasion - and it may not cost quite as much as you think. If you choose to gild the top of the cake but not the sides, you will only have to buy 1 x 25-leaf book of gold; you'll need 2 to encase the whole cake.

Place the cake on to its stand or serving plate.

The gold leaf needs to be applied very carefully in a room with no draughts. I find it easier to gild the sides of the cake first. Place the gold booklet close to the cake and slide off a sheet at a time, by gently holding the top 2 corners with the tips of the 2 paint brushes, using both your hands. Static will cause the bristles to grip on to the sheet. Try not to breathe on or touch the gold before it is on the cake!

With the tip of your finger, or using the back of a teaspoon, gently flatten the gold leaf on to the cake, then smooth it down with a brush.

If you would rather not use so much gilding, simply apply just 3 or 4 sheets, randomly laying them across the surface of the cake. The contrast of the dark chocolate and the gold looks stunning.

SERVES 16-20

1 x Chocolate Celebration Cake with Ganache (see p14)

30 sheets loose 23-carat gold leaf (it comes in a book of 25 sheets, each 8x8cm)
2 medium paint brushes

TO BAKE see: Chocolate Celebration Cake, p14

abstract expressionist

Transform your cake into a work of art! This cake is inspired by Jackson Pollock. We may not lay a huge sheet on the floor as he did, but we do have a small edible canvas covered in bright beetroot-coloured icing. Using a pastry brush and a piping bag, splatter and flick melted chocolate and icing all over the cake and release the artist in you. Ask the children to help, if you dare…

Turn the cake upside down on to a serving plate, so the flat base becomes the top.

Place the icing sugar in a bowl and gradually add the reserved beetroot juice from the cake recipe. If you would like a more shocking pink, you will need extra help from the food colour: drop a little of it (remembering it is very strong) into the icing sugar and stir until well blended and quite bright pink. Make sure you do not use too much, as the icing needs to remain thick enough to coat the back of a spoon. Pour it over the cake and allow to dry for at least 1 hour.

Place a small heatproof bowl over a saucepan of gently simmering water, making sure the base of the bowl does not touch the water. Add the white chocolate to the bowl and heat until it melts, stirring only very occasionally. Cool slightly, then spoon into a piping bag. Repeat with the dark chocolate. Snip the very ends of both bags. Dilute a little more pink food colour in a dribble of water, making sure it remains darker than the icing covering the cake.

Now for the fun bit: drizzle and flick both colours of chocolate all over your cake canvas, then shake over the pink colour using the pastry brush or toothbrush. Be as freeform as you like, until you have produced your very own edible masterpiece.

SERVES 10

1 x Chocolate and Beetroot Cake (see p21), with reserved beetroot juice

250g icing sugar, sifted
pink food colour (optional)
25g white chocolate, broken into pieces
25g dark chocolate, broken into pieces
2 piping bags
1 pastry brush or toothbrush

TO BAKE see: Chocolate and Beetroot Cake, p21

blackberry and geranium genoese

Sweet-scented geranium plants (Pelargonium, to be correct) are well worth hunting out. It's the oils in the leaves that make them special. Rub them between your fingers, or cook with them, and they release a wonderful scent and flavour: lemon, orange, peppermint, even nutmeg and cinnamon! Attar of Roses is my favourite. In season, why not follow Elizabeth David's advice and combine geranium with blackberry; they have an extraordinary affinity.

To make the syrup, chop 3 of the geranium leaves. Place all the ingredients (reserving the last whole geranium leaf) in a small saucepan and simmer until reduced to about 2 tbsp. Strain and leave to cool. Taste and add the whole geranium leaf if you like, or 1 tsp more rosewater, as you prefer. Allow to infuse for a day or so.

Space out the 12 geranium leaves evenly in the base of the prepared cake tin, then pour in the batter and bake as described (see p34). When the cake is cool, remove the papers and the leaves.

Slice in half horizontally and sprinkle the cut surfaces with the syrup. Fill with the cream filling and the blackberries. Sandwich together and dust the top with icing sugar. Decorate with more blackberries, sprigs of sweet geranium leaves and flowers.

SERVES 8

1 x Genoese Cake batter and
  cream filling, kept separate
  (see p34)

FOR THE SYRUP
4 sweet geranium leaves
3 tsp rosewater, or to taste
50g caster sugar
juice of half a lemon

12 young sweet geranium leaves
  (from one variety), plus more
  with flowers to decorate
250g blackberries, plus more to
  decorate
icing sugar, to dust

TO BAKE see: Genoese Sponge, p34

eastern fantasy

This enchanting cake has a branch of fabric hydrangea and berries with a little bird sitting in the foliage. Layered organza, velvet and bejewelled ribbons hug the sides.

Colour the sugarpaste the day before, making a pale pistachio green with the 3 food colour pastes (see p11).

To cover the cake with sugarpaste, remove any star anise flowers from the top and turn it upside down on a clean work surface, so the flat base is uppermost. Warm the jam gently in a small pan, then push it through a sieve and brush it all over the cake.

Dust a clean work surface and a rolling pin with icing sugar and roll out the sugarpaste into a circle slightly larger than the diameter of the cake and sides and no thinner than 5mm. Keep moving the sugarpaste and run a palette knife underneath it or dust with more icing sugar as necessary, as it is so frustrating if it sticks to the work surface.

Lift the sugarpaste on to the cake with your hands (or wrap it loosely around the rolling pin) and place it on the cake. Rub all over and smooth around the sides until you have a good shape, then cut away the excess sugarpaste. Run a palette knife under the cake and lift it on to the final plate, board or cake stand. Leave the icing to set for an hour or 2, if possible. It can be decorated straight away, but be careful not to dent the icing.

Using the royal icing, attach the branch to the top of the cake, and secure the 3 ribbons with a dab of royal icing at the back. Push the bird in among the flowers.

SERVES 8–10

1 x 20cm Star Anise, Almond and Clementine Cake (see p40) with syrup

1kg white sugarpaste
1 pot Sugarflair Eucalyptus food colour paste
1 pot Sugarflair Caramel/Ivory food colour paste
1 pot Sugarflair Mint Green food colour paste
3 tbsp apricot jam
icing sugar, to dust
50g bag white royal icing
branch of artificial intertwined berries and hydrangea
70cm 5.5cm-wide pale lilac organza ribbon
70cm 2cm-wide silver bejewelled ribbon
70cm 1.5cm-wide burgundy velvet ribbon
1 artificial bird, secured on a cocktail stick

TO BAKE see: Star Anise, Almond and Clementine Cake, p40

mosaic cake

Very striking designs can be made with simple, graphic patterns of sweets and chocolates. Here, the colour palette has been limited to give more impact. Children, especially, will love to create their own designs.

Turn the cake upside down and split in half horizontally. Spread most of the lime buttercream over the cut surface and place the other cake on top so the flat base becomes the top. Spread a very thin layer of the remaining buttercream around the sides (this will help the sugarpaste stick to the cake).

Roll out the sugarpaste on a clean board, lightly dusting both the board and a rolling pin with a little icing sugar to stop it sticking. Roll into a rough square about 5mm thick and slightly larger than the diameter of the cake and sides. Lift it with your hands or loosely roll it around the rolling pin, place it over the cake and gently smooth around the sides, rubbing it with your hands. Try not to stretch the sugarpaste and work as quickly as you can as it will dry out fairly quickly. Cut away any excess and, provided it is still clean, seal in a polythene bag; you can reuse it another time. Leave to dry for a few hours or, even better, overnight.

Using the royal icing, stick on the chocolate beans; it is a good idea to work out the pattern first on a board.

Finish by wrapping the ribbon around the cake and sticking down the seam at the back with a dab of royal icing.

SERVES 10

1 x Sticky Ginger Cake with
   Lime Buttercream (see p28),
   kept separate

1kg white sugarpaste
icing sugar, to dust
60g bag white royal icing
2 boxes chocolate beans
1m 2cm-wide spotted ribbon

TO BAKE see: Sticky Ginger Cake, p28

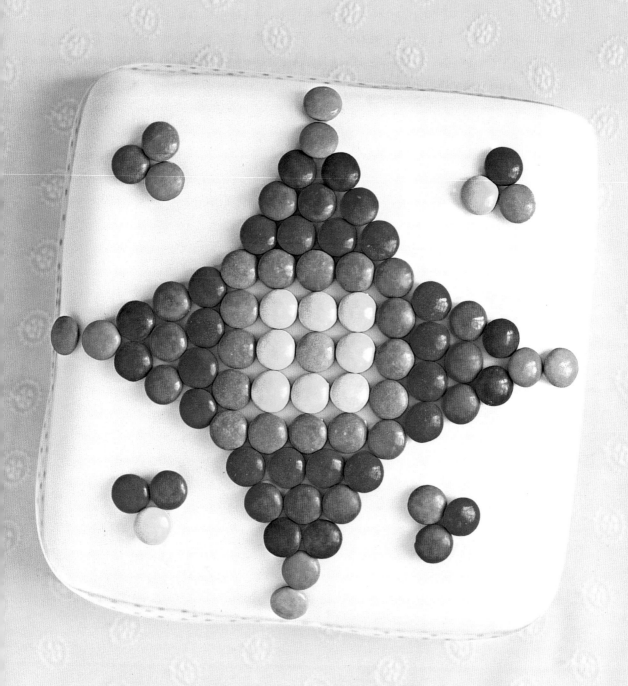

gala cake

Flags and bunting decorate this 4-tiered candy-striped cake. I have used fresh raspberry and blueberry fruit purees, lemon curd and lime to flavour the buttercream, but you could try strawberry, mango, passion fruit or blackcurrant purees, or even use good-quality jams to create each flavour instead. The bunting and flags can be made well ahead of time. I find it easiest to choose their colours first, then coordinate the buttercream colours to match.

For the flags, glue the scraps of ribbon and paper on to the cocktail sticks. To make the bunting, cut out paper triangles and glue them on to the ribbon.

Make the 4 coloured buttercreams. Divide the buttercream equally between 4 bowls. Make the raspberry puree by gently warming the fruits in a small saucepan, crushing with a fork, then sieving to remove the pips. Allow to cool. Make the blueberry puree in the same way, adding 1 tbsp water to the pan. Add the raspberry puree to 1 bowl of buttercream, the blueberry puree to another and the lemon curd to the third. Finally add the lime zest and juice and a little green food colour to the last.

Take the 4 Victoria sponges (or split them horizontally if you have chosen to bake 2 large cakes instead). Spread a different buttercream between each of the 4 layers, topping with the blueberry.

Place the cake on its stand. Arrange the flags and windmills over the top and attach the bunting to the stand with the sticky tape.

SERVES 16

2 x recipe Victoria Sponge
  (see p24)

tube of glue
scraps of contrasting ribbon and
  paper
8 cocktail sticks
180cm 5mm-wide ribbon
  (or enough to wrap twice round
  your cake stand)
1 x recipe vanilla Buttercream
  (see p9)
80g raspberries
80g blueberries
4 tbsp lemon curd
zest of 1 lime, finely grated, and
  juice of ½ lime
green food colour
2 paper windmills (optional)
1 roll double-sided sticky tape

TO BAKE see: Victoria Sponge, p24

summer cherries

It is said that you can trace old Roman roads in Britain by the wild cherry trees that grew up from stones spat out by legions as they marched! Here is a very simple cake decorated with cherry sweets as a tribute to them.

Place the cake flat base up on a clean board or work surface. Brush the jam all over it. Lightly dust a clean, flat surface with icing sugar (dust your rolling pin too) and roll out the sugarpaste into a rectangle no thinner than 5mm and slightly larger than the cake and sides.

Lift the sugarpaste with your hands or loosely roll it around the rolling pin, place it over the cake and gently smooth around the sides, covering the cake. Do not stretch the sugarpaste and work as quickly as you can, as it will dry out fairly quickly. Cut away any excess and, provided it is clean, seal it in a polythene bag for future use. Smooth the cake and sides all over with the palms of your hands; any lumps or bumps can hopefully be removed now.

Arrange the cherry sweets on the surface of the cake, sticking them on with a little royal icing. Attach the ribbon, again using the royal icing to adhere, at the back of the cake.

SERVES 8

1 x Cherry and Marzipan Cake (see p50), baked in a loaf tin

2 tbsp apricot jam, warmed and sieved
icing sugar, to dust
1kg white sugarpaste
6 cherry boiled sweets on stalks (see p207)
50g bag white royal icing
90cm 45mm-wide green or red gingham ribbon

TO BAKE see: Cherry and Marzipan Cake, p50

sweet shop

A feast for a child's eye (just don't expect the cake to be eaten first). Any selection of sweets can be used; pile them high! I have used the old-fashioned sorts that I used to buy on Saturdays as a child. My own children love them, too.

Place the cake on a clean board. Lightly dust a work top with icing sugar (dust your rolling pin, too) and roll out the sugarpaste into a circle no thinner than 5mm and slightly larger than the diameter of the cake and sides.

Lift the sugarpaste with your hands or loosely wrap it around the rolling pin, place it over the cake and gently smooth around the sides, covering the cake. Do not stretch the sugarpaste and work as quickly as you can, as it will dry out fairly quickly. Cut away any excess and seal it in a polythene food bag at room temperature for future use (providing it doesn't have fudge icing on it). Smooth the top and sides all over with the palms of your hands; any lumps, bumps or blemishes can hopefully be removed now.

Arrange the sweets randomly over the surface of the cake, with the jelly beans around the base, sticking them all on with the royal icing.

SERVES 8

1 x Family Chocolate Cake with Fudge Icing (see p17), iced over the top and sides

icing sugar, to dust
1kg white sugarpaste
a selection of sweets (I used 2 candy canes; 1 sugar mouse, 2 sweetie bracelets and 1 necklace; 1 small packet of sugar hearts; 6 striped marshmallows; 3–4 flying saucers; 40–50 jelly beans)
60g bag white royal icing

TO BAKE see: Family Chocolate Cake, p17

a summer garden

This is one of the simplest decorations in this book and shows a beautiful cake does not need to be complicated or time-consuming. Any seasonal, edible flowers could be used; try primroses, violets, chrysanthemums or daisies.

Preheat the oven to 170ºC/fan 150ºC/325ºF/gas mark 3. Scatter the pistachios on to a baking sheet and roast in the oven for about 5–10 minutes, shaking once and watching carefully to make sure they don't burn, then remove and chop.

Make a white chocolate ganache with the chocolate, cream and rosewater, using the method on p18 (this makes twice that amount).

Turn the cake upside down so the flat base becomes the top and split it in half. Fill with a layer of the ganache, then with the raspberries, and top with the second layer of cake. Spread the top and sides with the remaining ganache.

Press the roasted pistachios all around the side of the cake and, when ready to serve, decorate the top with the edible flowers tightly packed together. Stunning.

SERVES 8

1 x White Chocolate and Cardamom Rosewater Sponge (see p18), baked in a round tin

100g shelled unsalted pistachios
200g Swiss white chocolate, finely chopped
200ml double cream
3 tsp rosewater
250g fresh raspberries
40–50 whole edible flowers (I used cornflowers, pinks, nasturtiums, marigolds, borage and very small sunflowers)

TO BAKE see: White Chocolate and Cardamom Rosewater Sponge, p18

giant cupcake

Instead of making a batch of cupcakes, why not confuse everyone and make a monster! It is a little wasteful because of the need to shape the coffee cakes, but enjoy sampling as you sculpt them. Cook's treat!

Preheat the oven to 180°C/fan 170°C/350°F/gas mark 4. Lightly butter 2 x 15cm diameter, 7cm deep, round tins and line the bases with baking parchment. Pour the batter into the tins and bake for 30–35 minutes. Leave to cool completely, then put it in the freezer for about an hour (this makes it much easier to shape).

Take 1 cake and, with a very sharp knife, cut down the sides at an angle so that it is narrower at the base (to mimic a cupcake case). Slice the cake horizontally and fill with buttercream, spreading it on the top surface too. Take the second cake and place on top. Shape it into a dome, then slice it in half horizontally and fill with buttercream.

Spread a layer of buttercream around the sides of the bottom cake and put the remainder into the piping bag fitted with the star nozzle. Ice the top just as you would a small cupcake.

Arrange the chocolate fingers vertically all around the sides of the cake for the 'cupcake case', pressing them into the buttercream. Sprinkle the chocolate coffee beans over the cake and place the candle on top.

SERVES 10-12

1 x Coffee and Hazelnut Cake batter (see p37)

1 x recipe vanilla Buttercream (see p9)
nylon piping bag
large star nozzle
2 x 125g packets milk or dark chocolate fingers
20 chocolate-covered coffee beans
1 x 10cm cake candle

TO BAKE see: Coffee and Hazelnut Cake, p37

rose petal heart

An exquisite combination of white chocolate, cardamom, rosewater and raspberries. This cake is temptingly strewn with crystallised petals and white chocolate curls; both can be made a few days ahead, then stored in dry conditions in a cardboard box at room temperature.

Split the cake, spoon in the filling and the fresh raspberries, then turn it upside down on to a cake stand. Place the icing sugar into a bowl and gradually add the rosewater, mixing all the time until the icing is thick enough to coat the back of a spoon. Pour over the cake and let it drizzle down the sides. Allow to set for an hour or so.

To make the chocolate curls, place a small heatproof bowl over a saucepan of gently simmering water, making sure the base of the bowl does not touch the water. Add the white chocolate to the bowl and heat until it melts, stirring only very occasionally. Pour it on to a plastic board, or a piece of marble, and spread out with a palette knife. Allow to set; a short spell in the refrigerator will help.

Run a sharp fine knife at a 45-degree angle across the chocolate (or use a vegetable peeler) and it will curl. Too cold and it won't work; too soft and it will need 15 minutes or so back in the refrigerator. You'll have to experiment.

Scatter the cake with the chocolate curls, then with the rose petals.

SERVES

1 x heart-shaped White Chocolate and Cardamom Rosewater Sponge with filling, kept separate (see p18)

250g fresh raspberries
200g icing sugar, sifted
2–2½ tbsp rosewater
100g white chocolate, broken into pieces
12 crystallised pink rose petals (see p107)

TO BAKE see: White Chocolate and Cardamom Rosewater Sponge, p18

pansy wreath

This enchanting cake is so summery with its circlet of violas and pansies. In spring it would look equally pretty decorated with crystallised primulas.

Place the cake upside down on to your serving plate or cake stand.

Tip the icing sugar into a small bowl and add 1½–2 tbsp water and a tiny amount of purple food colour. The icing should be thick enough to coat the back of a spoon. Spoon it over the cake and allow it to drizzle down the sides.

Arrange the violas and pansies in a circle, using the royal icing to affix them, if you like, then place a few in the middle of the cake. It's as simple as that.

SERVES 6

1 x Very Lemony Crunch Cake
   with syrup (see p31)

150g icing sugar, sifted
purple food colour
20–25 crystallised small violas
   and pansies (see p107)
50g bag white royal icing
   (optional)

TO BAKE see: Very Lemony Crunch Cake, p31

how to make crystallised flowers and leaves

A quick and stunning decoration that requires very little equipment, just a quiet hour and a bit of patience. These should keep for up to 1 week in a dry place. Use unsprayed flowers that are completely dry.

Line a baking sheet with baking parchment.

Place the egg white in a bowl and the sugar in another. Hold the flower, petal or leaf at the base and paint with egg, ensuring you cover every fold. Gently sprinkle on the sugar, again making sure every surface is covered, then shake off the excess.

If crystallising whole roses, push a fine florists' wire through the base of the bloom, then hook the wire over a tall glass. Leave overnight in a dry, warm place. The flower will dry while hanging.

Lay petals or leaves on the lined sheet and leave overnight in a dry, warm place (an airing cupboard is ideal). They will harden in a few hours, becoming brittle.

Store in an airtight container, lined and interleaved with baking parchment. They are very fragile, so only make a couple of layers.

MAKES AS MANY AS YOU WANT

egg white, lightly whisked
white caster sugar
edible flowers and leaves,
    such as whole roses or rose
    petals, violas, pansies, violets,
    mimosa, cowslips, pinks,
    primroses, lavender, sweet
    geranium leaves, mint leaves
small paint brush
florists' wire (optional)

rose garden

This is the cake to celebrate high summer, when the days are long, the sun is high in the sky and the scent of fresh-mown grass is in the air. Summoning up memories of lazy afternoon teas in the garden, and adorned with full-blown crystallised roses, it's a magical cake.

Invert the cake on to a cake stand or plate, so that the flat base forms the top surface.

Sift the icing sugar into a bowl and gradually add the orange juice, mixing all the time until it is thick enough to coat the back of the spoon. Pour over the cake, letting it drizzle down the sides.

Allow to set for at least 1 hour, then carefully arrange the crystallised roses in the centre.

SERVES 8

1 x Pistachio and Orange
   Blossom Cake (see p38),
   with its syrup

200g icing sugar
2–2½ tbsp orange juice
3 crystallised roses (see p107)

TO BAKE see: Pistachio and Orange Blossom Cake, p38

easter chocolate truffle cake

If you haven't already eaten too many chocolate eggs, this would be a perfect ending to Easter lunch, or served at tea time. The sugar eggs can be made weeks ahead, and the cake a day or 2 in advance then assembled shortly before serving.

To make the sugar eggs, place the caster sugar in a bowl. Mix in 5–10ml water and mix; it will feel a bit like wet sand. Pack it into the egg mould, levelling off with a palette knife, and allow to set for about 24 hours; the eggs will have hardened.

Turn the mould upside down and lightly tap on a work surface. The half-eggs should drop out. Stick the halves together with a little white royal icing. Decorate by sticking on the sugar flowers, ribbon roses or bows with royal icing, then pipe on little yellow polka dots.

When you are ready to eat, place the cake on to a serving plate or cake stand. Arrange the decorated eggs in a circle with the foliage.

SERVES 12

1 x Dark Chocolate Mousse Cake (see p58)

100g white caster sugar
1 plastic egg mould (makes 9 sugar eggs, each 3cm long)
50g bag white royal icing
selection of tiny sugar flowers, ribbon roses and little bows
50g bag yellow royal icing
fresh (preferably edible) foliage

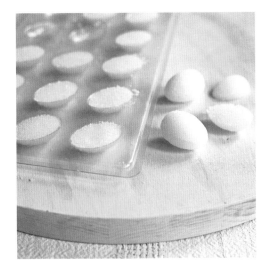

TO BAKE see: Dark Chocolate Mousse Cake, p58

maypole

For centuries an expression of joy and hope celebrating the start of spring. You could even cover the whole cake with a carpet of sugar flowers. I have specified the ribbons I used, but do take these instructions only as a guide.

To make the maypole, twist the white ribbon all around the tube tightly and glue at both ends. Next, take the 6 lengths of coloured 3mm ribbon and, starting at one end, wind them together tightly round and round the tube. Again, the ribbons need to be fastened at the bottom of the pole (I took them inside the tube and glued firmly). At the top end, secure them inside the pole, then cascade them out.

Make a tassel for the top by taking 2 x 15cm lengths of each of the 6 coloured 3mm ribbons, tying together very firmly and wedging into the top of the pole. Tie 6 tiny bows in different colours, using about 15cm each of the 3mm ribbons.

Now, turn the cake upside down, split it horizontally and sandwich with some of the buttercream. Place the other half on top so the flat base is uppermost, then spread buttercream over the top and sides.

Lightly dust a clean, flat surface with icing sugar (dust your rolling pin too) and roll out the sugarpaste into a circle no thinner than 5mm and slightly larger than the diameter of the cake and sides. Lift the sugarpaste with your hands or loosely roll it around the rolling pin, place it over the cake and gently smooth around the sides, covering the cake. Cut away any excess and smooth the cake all over with your hands; any lumps or bumps can be removed now.

Find the centre of the cake and push in the maypole, piping a little royal icing into the hole to secure. Take the 6 cascading ribbons from the top of the pole and, using royal icing, secure at 6 equidistant points at both the edge and base of the cake. Cut away any excess. Stick a little contrasting bow at the 6 points around the cake and attach the flowered ribbon around the base. Adhere the sugar flowers round the bottom of the maypole, again using the royal icing as 'glue'.

TO BAKE see: Orange Drizzle Cake, p32

SERVES 8

1 x Orange Drizzle Cake (see p32)
½ x recipe orange Buttercream (see p9)

1m 10mm-wide white satin ribbon
1 plastic or cardboard tube, about 15cm long and 1cm in diameter
1 pot glue
6 x 120cm lengths 3mm-wide ribbon in different colours
icing sugar, to dust
1kg white sugarpaste
50g bag white royal icing
70cm 10cm-wide ribbon (mine was green with white flowers)
5 small sugar flowers

summer berry
rose-scented meringue

All the aromas, flavours and colours of summer. Tiers
of crisp, candy-striped meringue with a marshmallowy
centre, oozing with a subtle rose-vanilla cream, packed
with berries and strewn with rose petals.

Spread out the 3 circles of meringue as described on p55. Dip the end
of a skewer, or a teaspoon handle, into the pink food colour (if using
food colour paste, dilute with a very little water first) and swirl over
the meringue. Bake as described on p55. The circles should be crispy
and dry on the outside and may be a bit cracked, which is fine. Leave
the oven door slightly ajar and allow to cool completely.

Whip the cream until soft peaks form, adding the vanilla, rosewater
and sugar, to taste. Place the largest meringue circle on a cake stand
or serving plate. Spread with some cream, sprinkle over some
berries, add a little more cream, then place the medium meringue on
top. Repeat with the remaining cream and berries and top with the
smallest disc. Dust with icing sugar and a little glitter, if liked, and
throw over the rose petals, letting them fall casually on and around.

SERVES 12

FOR THE MERINGUE
1 x Exotic Fruit Chewy Meringue
   (see p55), unbaked

1 pot pink food colour paste or
   liquid food colour

FOR THE FILLING
600ml double cream
2 tsp vanilla extract, or seeds
   from 1 vanilla pod
2 tsp rosewater
4 tbsp icing sugar, plus more
   to dust (optional)
800g berries of your choice:
   raspberries, blueberries,
   redcurrants, blackcurrants,
   blackberries, sliced
   strawberries and cherries
1 pot clear edible glitter
   (optional)
15–20 rose petals

TO BAKE see: Exotic Fruit Chewy Meringue, p55

pink iced heart

What more does a girl need for a special celebration? This is simplicity itself to make.

Preheat the oven to 180°C/fan 170°C/350°F gas mark 4.

Butter well a large heart-shaped tin, 23cm at its widest part, and line the base with baking parchment. Pour in the batter and bake for 30–35 minutes. When a skewer inserted into the centre comes out clean, it is ready. Leave to cool slightly in the tin, then turn out on to a wire rack, remove the paper and allow to become completely cold.

Make the buttercream by beating the butter, icing sugar and vanilla for 5 minutes until really soft and fluffy. Add drops of the pink food colour. Any shade is fine: you can pick a baby pink, a medium or, as we did for this photograph, a strong, full-on girlie tone.

Turn the cake upside down, split it horizontally and, using a palette knife, spread some of the pink buttercream over the cut surface, then add a layer of jam. Place the other half of the cake on top and spread the rest of the buttercream all over the top and sides, making it as smooth as possible.

Straight away, press a collar of the dragees all around the outside edge (the icing will start to set if you leave it) and sprinkle them all with a little glitter. Finish by placing the candles on the cake, if you like.

SERVES 8

1 x Victoria Sponge batter (see p24)

250g unsalted butter, plus more for the tin
300g icing sugar, sifted
1 tsp vanilla extract
pink food colour
3 tbsp raspberry or strawberry jam
2 x 30g packets multicoloured dragees (I added a few larger and tiny silver dragees, but it's fine to use all one size)
1 pot clear edible glitter
3 pink or purple candles and candle holders (optional)

TO BAKE see: Victoria Sponge, p24

party cake with streamers

Perfect for all ages. The little 'cakes' on top are made out of sugar. You can make them a few weeks ahead if you like; store in a cardboard box at room temperature.

Place the chocolate cake on to the board. To make the little cakes, simply place a disc of sugarpaste into each case. Make up a small amount of icing by very gradually adding 2 tbsp water to the icing sugar until it is thick enough to coat the back of a spoon, then divide between 3 bowls. Colour the first pink, another green and the third yellow. Spoon into the paper cases, making 4 of each colour, then top with the coloured sprinkles. Arrange them on the cake.

Curl the ribbons by running the blade of a blunt knife along the length of each, then lay these streamers casually over the cake, allowing them to cascade down the sides.

SERVES 8

1 x Family Chocolate Cake with Fudge Icing (see p17), iced over the top and sides

1 x 25cm decorative foil board
120g white sugarpaste
12 foil petit four cases
200g icing sugar, sifted
pink food colour
green food colour
yellow food colour
3 tsp coloured sprinkles (¼ tsp per cake)
3–4 rolls metallic ribbon, each cut into 1m strips

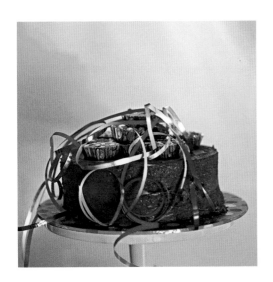

TO BAKE see: Family Chocolate Cake, p17

ribbon roses

These roses are very quick and easy and there's no sewing.
I used realistic colours but yours can be in crazy shades, if
you prefer. They can, of course, be made months ahead.

Colour the sugarpaste the day before, if possible (see p11). I made a
clotted cream tone, using the 2 shades listed here.

Warm the jam gently in a pan, sieve it and brush all over the cake.
Dust a clean work surface with icing sugar and roll out the sugarpaste
into a circle roughly as big as the diameter and sides of the cake, and
no thinner than 5mm. Keep moving the sugarpaste and run a palette
knife underneath it, adding more icing sugar if necessary. Lift the
sugarpaste on to the cake with your hands, smooth it all over and cut
away any excess. Run a palette knife under the cake and lift it on to
your final cake stand or plate. Leave to set for at least an hour or so.

To make a ribbon rose, take 1m of wired ribbon and, as close as
possible to one end, tie a small tight knot. From the other end, pull
the wire out; the ribbon will ruffle. Ease it along towards the knotted
end. Keep pulling on the wire gently until all the ribbon is ruffled.
Starting at the knot end, twist the ruffled ribbon round and round the
knot to form the central bud and 'petals'. Secure with
the wire tightly around the base and cut off any excess.
Repeat with the other 2 ribbons.

Wrap the organza ribbon around the cake and attach
with a dab of royal icing at the back. Stick the ribbon
roses in the centre and tuck in the artificial leaves.

SERVES 8

1 x Cherry and Marzipan Cake
  (see p50), baked in a round tin

1kg white sugarpaste
1 pot peach and/or 1 pot
  primrose food colour paste
3 tbsp apricot jam
icing sugar, to dust
3 x 1m lengths 38mm-wide wired
  ribbon, in different colours
80cm 35mm-wide green organza
  ribbon
50g bag white royal icing
3 artificial leaves

TO BAKE see: Cherry and Marzipan Cake, p50

fresh petal confetti cake

No special equipment, time or expertise required, but serve it soon after decorating, or the petals start to wilt. The only secret is in your choice of edible petals. I used cornflowers, lavender, rose petals and marigolds. I filled and covered the cake with Lavender and Lemon Buttercream (see p146), but plain lemon or vanilla Buttercream (see p9) is just as good.

If you have chosen to bake in 2 tins, place the bottom half of the sponge on a work surface and spread with the lemon curd and a layer of buttercream. If you have made just 1 deeper cake, split it horizontally with a serrated knife, invert the top half on a work surface and spread with the lemon curd and a layer of buttercream. Top with the remaining sponge, inverted so the flat base is uppermost, and cover the top and sides with buttercream. Try to make it as smooth as possible.

Roll up the petals (not the lavender as they are tiny flowers) and slice very finely into strips with a sharp knife, or snip with a pair of scissors. Keep the petals fresh for an hour or so, if needed, by laying them out on a damp cloth or kitchen towel.

When ready to decorate, take a small handful of petals at a time and press into the buttercream all around the sides of the cake. To finish, scatter the remaining petal confetti on top.

SERVES 8-10

1 x Victoria Sponge (see p24)

5 tbsp good-quality lemon curd
½ x recipe Lemon and Lavender Buttercream (see p146)
selection of unsprayed edible petals in contrasting colours: try lavender, cornflowers, rose petals, marigolds, chrysanthemums, pansies, sunflowers, primulas, daisies, carnations or pinks

TO BAKE see: Victoria Sponge, p24

fluttering butterflies

Exquisite fabric and feather butterflies on wires are widely available in an assortment of colours and designs and will fly over your cake to give instant impact.

Colour the sugarpaste the day before, if possible, using the 2 listed food colours, until you have achieved your desired shade (see p11).

Gently warm the jam, sieve it, then brush all over the cake. Dust a clean work surface with icing sugar and roll out the sugarpaste into a circle roughly the diameter of the cake and sides and no thinner than 5mm. Keep moving the sugarpaste and run a palette knife underneath it, adding a little icing sugar if necessary. Lift the sugarpaste on to the cake with your hands (or wrap loosely around the rolling pin) and place it on the cake. Rub all over and smooth around the side until you have a good shape, then cut away any excess sugarpaste.

Run a knife under the cake and lift on to your final cake stand or plate. If you wish to press a blossom pattern into the sugarpaste, then push the cutter into the cake top and sides about 30 times. Leave to set for at least an hour or 2 if you can.

Wrap the ribbons loosely around the cake, twining them together, and tie at the back or cut neatly and stick with a little royal icing. Twist all the butterfly wires together and attach to the ribbons at the back of the cake. Bend the wires over the cake so the butterflies appear to be fluttering above it.

SERVES 8

1 x Cherry and Marzipan Cake
  (see p50), baked in a round tin

1kg white sugarpaste
1 pot tangerine/apricot food
  colour paste
1 pot claret food colour paste
3 tbsp apricot jam
icing sugar, to dust
1 x 1cm blossom cutter (optional)
2 x 1m 38mm-wide ribbons
  in contrasting colours to
  coordinate with the butterflies
1m 15mm-wide braided ribbon
50g bag white royal icing
  (optional)
6–8 butterflies on wires (mine
  were about 8cm wide)

TO BAKE see: Cherry and Marzipan Cake, p50

bollywood extravaganza

This exotic cake is inspired by my yearly visits to India. Its dazzling array of sugarpaste full-blown roses in clashing colours reminds me of sizzling–hot spices. Even if your roses are not perfect, their sheer impact in these vibrant colours, dusted with glitter and encircled with bejewelled ribbon, will create a stunning centrepiece.

The roses can be made a few weeks ahead. Divide the sugarpaste into 5 blocks (this quantity makes about 40 x 5cm roses).

When colouring the sugarpaste, the use of black is optional. It does make a more interesting colour, but use literally a pinprick when required. Mix all the 5 colours (see p11). Create a deep red with poppy red, egg yellow and liquorice black; a bright pink with claret, pink and liquorice black; a light pink with claret; a bright orange with poppy red and egg yellow; a lighter orange with primrose, egg yellow and liquorice black. Allow the sugarpaste to rest overnight (it will be much easier to mould).

Make 8 roses in each colour (see p129). Sprinkle with glitter and store in a covered box at room temperature.

When ready to assemble, place the cake on to the serving plate. Arrange the roses all over the top.

Finish by wrapping the ribbon around the cake, using a blob of extra Ganache at the back to hold it in place.

TO BAKE see: Chocolate Celebration Cake, p14

SERVES 16-20

1 x 30cm Chocolate Celebration Cake with Ganache (see p14) made with chilli-flavoured chocolate

1.2kg white sugarpaste
1 pot Sugarflair Poppy Red food colour paste
1 pot Sugarflair Egg Yellow food colour paste
1 pot Sugarfair Liquorice food colour paste (optional)
1 pot Sugarflair Claret food colour paste
1 pot Sugarflair Pink food colour paste
1 pot Sugarflair Primrose food colour paste
1 pot clear edible glitter
100cm of 4cm-wide ribbon, bejewelled or ornate if possible

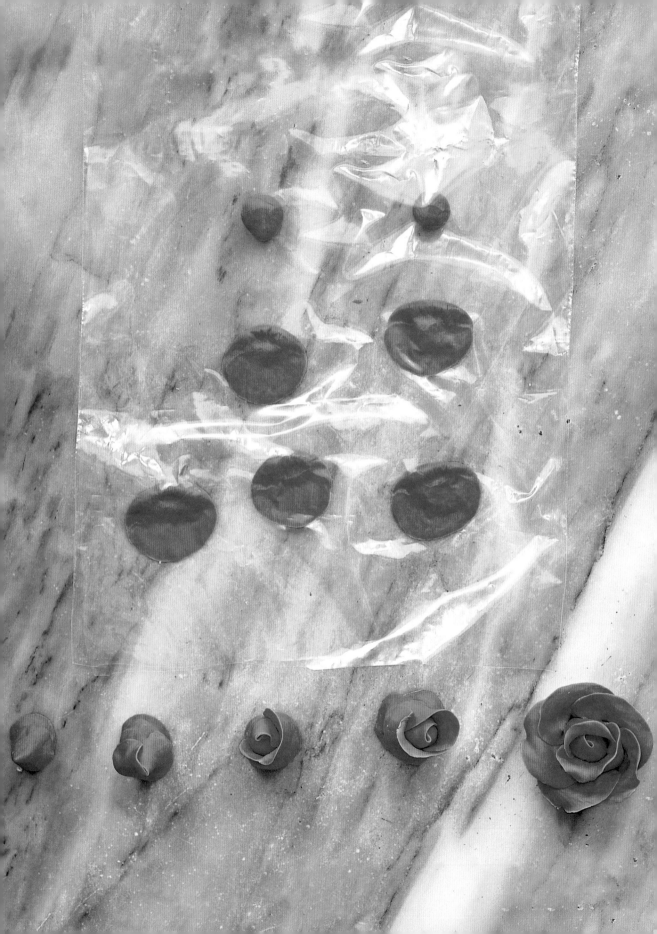

how to make sugarpaste roses

It is well worth mastering how to make these; don't worry, I have never met anyone who can't! It requires no special equipment, just a bit of patience and perseverance. In nature no 2 roses are the same, and chances are yours won't be either. As you become more experienced you'll find it easier, and your roses will very quickly improve.

The darker the sugarpaste – and hence the more food colour paste you have used – the softer it will be, and harder to mould. So, for your first attempts, use pale colours. (Using liquid food colour may make it too soft.) Once you have kneaded and coloured the sugarpaste (see p11) you may need to adjust the texture: if it is too soft, add a little icing sugar; if too dry, add a tiny amount of white vegetable fat. If possible, colour the sugarpaste the day before you need it, as it will be much easier to work. Store sugarpaste in a sealed polythene bag, and finished roses in a cardboard box (not an airtight container or they will sweat), both at room temperature. Never keep them in the refrigerator. Sugarpaste roses will keep for months.

Take 40g of the sugarpaste. Split a polythene bag open and place on a flat work top. Tear off one-third of the sugarpaste and roll it into a ball in your hands, then into a cone. Flatten the base on to your work surface, then indent it to shape a cone on top of a rough ball.

Mould 7 or 8 balls (to become the petals) from the remaining sugarpaste and lay them on one side of the bag. Fold over the other side on top and flatten each ball until quite thin. The thinner it is, the finer the petal, but don't be too ambitious at first.

Very gently peel back the polythene. Take a petal at a time and, with the side you pressed on uppermost, mould it around the cone, competely covering the top. Take the second petal and place it centrally over the seam of the first (again, with the side you pressed on uppermost), moulding it around the cone. Place the third petal directly opposite. Tweak out all the petals as you work, to look like a real rose. You have now made a rosebud!

Fold the remaining 4 or 5 petals around the rosebud in the same way, each overlapping the last. Again, tweak out these petals as you work. With a small knife, cut away the base at a slight angle. You can use these offcuts when you make the next rose.

MAKES AS MANY AS YOU WANT

40g sugarpaste for each rose
icing sugar, to dust
tiny knob of white vegetable fat

christmas trees

A little forest of sugarpaste trees with candy cane trunks and sparkling sugar snow adorn this easy-to-make cake.

Colour 300g of the sugarpaste 2 shades of green, making the darker tone first (see p11). Seal in separate polythene bags. Turn the cake upside down on to a serving plate, securing with a dab of jam. If there are any holes or the cake is a slightly dodgy shape, correct it now with bits of marzipan. Once you're happy, gently warm the remaining jam in a small pan, then sieve and brush all over the cake. Knead the marzipan until pliable. Dust a work surface and rolling pin with icing sugar and roll out the marzipan into a circle slightly larger than the top and sides of the cake, about 5mm thick. Lift on to the cake, smoothing all over, and cut away any excess. Leave overnight to firm up.

Brush the marzipan with the brandy and, on a clean, flat surface, knead the remaining white sugarpaste until pliable. Dust a work surface and rolling pin with icing sugar and roll out the sugarpaste in a circle about 5mm thick and slightly larger than the diameter of the cake and sides. Lift with your hands (or loosely wrap around the rolling pin) and place over the cake. Gently smooth with your hands and cut away any excess. Again, leave overnight to harden.

For the trees, roll out the darker green sugarpaste to about 7mm thick and cut out 1 large and 5 small trees. Repeat with the lighter green, cutting 2 large and 4 smaller trees. Dip all their edges into the glitter then, with the royal icing, stick them on the candy canes. Re-roll the 2 green sugarpastes to 2mm thick and cut out 1 large and 5 small trees in darker green and 2 large and 4 small trees in light green. Stick these on to the backs of the trees, to hide the join to the candy canes. Push the 'trunks' into the cake, all facing the same way. Break up the sugar cubes and scatter over the surface, then sprinkle with glitter. Finish by twisting the ribbon round the cake about 6 times and attaching at the back with the royal icing.

TO BAKE see: Rich Tamarind Fruit Cake, p46

MAKES 40 SLICES

1 x Rich Tamarind Fruit Cake (see p46)

1.3kg white sugarpaste
1 pot green food colour paste
25cm round cake drum (optional)
4 tbsp apricot jam
1kg marzipan (see p138)
icing sugar, to dust
15ml brandy or boiled water
1 large red-and-white candy cane, cut into 6mm lengths
7cm tree cutter
3.5cm tree cutter
1 pot clear edible glitter
50g bag white royal icing
2–3 sugar cubes
4.5m 3mm-wide red satin ribbon

glacé fruit and nut cake

The most wonderful jewel-like glacé fruits - whole pears, clementines and figs - appear in good food halls towards Christmas. I specify which fruits and nuts I used, but please alter this to your preference and use what you can find. This cake is a truly stunning centrepiece for the festive season, and not a plastic robin in sight. Please make sure the bay leaves don't get eaten!

Turn the cake over, so that the flat base is uppermost. Place the jam and rum in a small pan and bring to the boil. Allow to cool a little, sieve and brush half over the top of the cake.

Roll out the marzipan to 10mm thick, using a little icing sugar on the work top and rolling pin. Using the tin as a guide, cut out a square the same size as the cake with a sharp knife. Lay it on top.

Brush the marzipan with more of the jam mixture and stud the fruits and nuts all over the surface of the cake, pushing them in so they don't fall off. Tuck the bay leaves in amongst them.

Entwine the raffia around the cake and tie with a knot. If it is not to be eaten for a few days, place a strip of baking parchment underneath the raffia to keep the sides from drying out.

MAKES 20 SLICES

1 x Tropical Fruit Cake without
   nuts on top (see p44)

3 tbsp apricot jam
2 tbsp rum
600g marzipan (see p138)
icing sugar, to dust
3 glacé pears
1 glacé clementine
3 glacé figs
6 slices glacé orange
12 whole glacé cherries
60 shelled unsalted pistachios
40 pecans
1 sprig of bay leaves
1.5m coloured raffia

TO BAKE see: Tropical Fruit Cake, p44

penguin cake

Originally designed as an alternative Christmas cake, there's no reason not to make this at any time. The penguins need to be kept at room temperature and the cake should not be hours out of the refrigerator or it will become difficult to cut, so decorate shortly before you serve it. The penguins can be made a few weeks ahead and stored in a lidded cardboard box (not an airtight container or tin as they will sweat).

To make the 'snow', add 1½–2 tbsp water to the icing sugar and mix until it is thick enough to coat the back of a spoon. Drizzle all over the top of the cake.

For each penguin, make a cone of black sugarpaste (the largest I made were 4cm tall and the smallest 2.5cm). Snip out 2 wings with the tip of a pair of scissors, and ease them away from the body. Roll out a little ball of white sugarpaste with your fingers, squash it flat to form the tummy and press on to the penguin, adhering with a little royal icing. Pipe 2 little eyes in white, allow to dry for an hour or so, then pipe in the black centres. Finish by piping a yellow beak. Make snowballs by rolling different-sized balls of white sugarpaste.

Decorate the cake by placing the penguins over and around it, adding the snowballs and, finally, the glitter for sparkle.

SERVES 12

1 x Surprise Fridge Cake
  (see p56)

150g icing sugar
250g black sugarpaste
50g white sugarpaste
20g bag white royal icing
20g bag black royal icing
20g bag yellow royal icing
1 pot clear edible glitter

TO BAKE see: Surprise Fridge Cake, p56

gingerbread man cake

A great classic Christmas cake for all the family; there's always someone who doesn't like fruit cake, so they can eat the gingerbread men!

Turn the cake upside down on to a cake stand. A dab of apricot jam will stop it moving around. If there are any holes or the cake is a dodgy shape, correct it now with little bits of marzipan. Once you are happy, brush all over with jam. Knead the marzipan until pliable. Dust a work surface with icing sugar and, using a little more on the rolling pin, roll the marzipan into a rough circle slightly larger than the top and sides of the cake and about 5mm thick. Lift on to the cake, smoothing all over, and cut off any excess. Leave overnight to firm up.

Brush the marzipan with the brandy and, on a clean, flat surface, knead the sugarpaste until pliable. Dust the work surface and rolling pin with icing sugar and roll out the sugarpaste in a rough circle about 5mm thick and slightly larger than the diameter of the cake and sides. Lift the sugarpaste with your hands (or loosely wrap it around the rolling pin) and place it over the cake. Gently smooth with your hands and cut away any excess. Leave overnight to harden.

Preheat the oven to 180°C/fan 170°C/350°F/gas mark 4. Roll the gingerbread dough out to 4mm thick and cut out 12 large and 12 small men. Line 2 baking sheets with baking parchment and lay out the shapes; smaller on 1 tray (they take less time to bake) and larger on the other. Press 2 cocktail sticks on to the backs of the legs of 3 smaller men so they will stand up later. Bake for 8–15 minutes, depending on size. The gingerbread will darken. Remove from the oven and cool on a wire rack. Pipe black eyes and red mouths on the large men and stick on red mini bean noses. Pipe black eyes and red noses and mouths on the small. Stick 3 buttons on the large men and 2 on the small. Surround the cake with the larger men, propped against it, dabbing their heads with a little royal icing to adhere. Carefully position the 3 men on sticks on the top of the cake. You will have 9 little men left over to serve separately.

TO BAKE see: Rich Tamarind Fruit Cake, p46; Gingerbread, p73

MAKES 40 SLICES

1 x Rich Tamarind Fruit Cake (see p46)
½ x batch Gingerbread dough (see p73)

4 tbsp apricot jam, warmed and sieved
1kg marzipan (see p138)
1 tbsp brandy or boiled water
icing sugar, to dust
1kg sugarpaste
6cm gingerbread man cutter
9cm gingerbread man cutter
6 cocktail sticks
30g bag black royal icing
30g bag red royal icing
60g bag white royal icing
bag of mini chocolate beans

marzipan criss-cross

Perfect for a winter's tea time.

Place the cake upside down on to a cake stand or serving plate. Warm the jam gently in a small pan, sieve, then brush over the top of the cake. On a clean work top dusted with icing sugar, roll out the marzipan to 10mm thick and the exact size of the top of the cake, using the tin as a guide. Trim the edges with a sharp knife, then lift the marzipan on to the cake. With the back of a long knife, indent the top, making the first indent exactly from one corner to the other and then marking parallel lines either side, each about 8cm apart. Repeat in the other direction to form a criss-cross. Wherever the lines meet, press a gold dragee into the marzipan.

To gild the 4 walnuts, mix the alcohol with the gold powder using the brush and paint the walnuts. Place them firmly at each corner of the cake (you may need royal icing to hold them in place). Entwine the raffia around the cake and tie with a knot. If it is not to be eaten for a few days, place a strip of baking parchment underneath the raffia to keep the sides from drying out.

marzipan

MAKES ABOUT 600G, ENOUGH TO COVER A 20CM CAKE

In a bowl, mix the icing sugar and almonds. In another bowl, mix the lemon juice, egg yolks and almond essence. Add the egg mixture gradually to the icing sugar and almonds and knead everything just until it forms a stiff paste. (It will become oily if overworked.) Store in a polythene bag in the refrigerator (use within a week).

SERVES 15

1 x Whisky, Date and Walnut
Cake (see p49), baked in a
square tin

2 tbsp apricot jam
icing sugar, to dust
600g marzipan (see recipe below)
50 gold dragees
4 walnut halves
½ tsp colourless alcohol
(vodka or gin)
edible gold powder
small paint brush
1 x 30g bag white royal icing
(optional)
1.5m natural raffia

190g icing sugar
380g ground almonds
3 tsp lemon juice
3 egg yolks
4 drops almond essence

TO BAKE see: Whisky, Date and Walnut Cake, p49

vintage glamour wedding cake

A beautiful 3-tiered timeless classic, this could take centre stage at any wedding feast. It can be baked and decorated at least a month in advance and there are no colours to mix as the entire scheme is in cream sugarpaste with highlights of gold. (You could also make this cake in white and gold.) If you break down each stage, giving yourself plenty of time, you may find it easier than you think.

the nuts and bolts

Thin cake boards are used only while you are assembling the cakes, and really serve to save your work surfaces, so you can use any board you have, even plywood. Cake drums, on the other hand, will support each tier of the finished cake, so must be bought for the purpose.

Prepare the cake tins and batter (see p46). Divide the batter between the tins, filling each to the same depth. Bake as instructed on p46. The smallest cake will take about 1¾ hours, the medium 2½–3 hours and the largest about 3 hours: if a skewer inserted into the centre comes out clean, it is ready. Leave to cool in the tins. When cold, prick all over with a fine skewer and sprinkle in the brandy. Wrap in baking parchment, then foil, until ready to use. You can continue to feed the cakes with 1–2 tbsp brandy every other week, for a month or 2.

to marzipan the cakes

Take the 20cm thin board and place the 15cm drum on it. Brush 1 tbsp apricot jam into the centre, then place the 15cm cake on top, upside down so the flat base forms the surface. If it is slightly smaller than the drum, make a strip of marzipan as wide as the side of the cake and the same circumference, and stick it to the edge. Similarly, all cakes should be the same height. If not, apply an extra-thin marzipan layer to the top of the shallow cake (use the tin as a guide). Repeat for the other cakes, placing the 20cm cake on the same-size drum and 25cm board, and the 25cm cake on the same-size drum and 30cm board.

Brush the 15cm cake with jam and knead 800g of marzipan until pliable. Dust the work surface and a rolling pin with icing sugar, and roll out into a rough square slightly larger than the top and sides of the cake and drum and about 5mm thick. Lift on to the cake and drum, smooth all over and cut away any excess. Cover the other 2 cakes the same way, using 1kg marzipan each. Leave overnight to firm up.

SERVES ABOUT 120–150

FOR THE CAKES
1 x 15cm diameter, 7cm deep, square cake tin
1 x 20cm diameter, 7cm deep, square cake tin
1 x 25cm diameter, 7cm deep, square cake tin
2 x Rich Tamarind Fruit Cake batter (see p46)
6 tbsp brandy
250g apricot jam, gently warmed and pushed through a sieve
3kg marzipan (see p138)
icing sugar, to dust

FOR THE BOARDS AND DRUMS
1 x 20cm square thin board
1 x 25cm square thin board
1 x 30cm square thin board
1 x 15cm diameter, 1cm thick, square cake drum
1 x 20cm diameter, 1cm thick, square cake drum
1 x 25cm diameter, 1cm thick, square cake drum

assembly

to cover the base drum

Dust the 30cm drum with icing sugar and sprinkle with a small amount of water. Knead 1kg of the sugarpaste until pliable, then dust a work surface and rolling pin with icing sugar and roll it into a rough square slightly larger than the top of the drum and about 3mm thick. Wrap it loosely around the rolling pin and lift on to the drum. Smooth with your hands and trim away any excess overhanging the sides. Replace the excess in a polythene bag and seal. Leave to dry overnight.

to cover the cakes

The 15cm cake will need about 800g of sugarpaste, and the 2 larger cakes about 1kg each. Work on just 1 cake at a time. For each cake, brush brandy all over the marzipan. This helps the sugarpaste to stick and is also an antiseptic. Lightly dust a clean surface with icing sugar and roll out the sugarpaste into a rough square about 5mm thick and slightly larger than the diameter of the cakes, its sides, and the drums.

Lift the sugarpaste with your hands, place it over the cake and gently smooth, covering the cake and drum. Do not stretch, and work as quickly as you can, as it will dry out. Cut away any excess, provided it is still clean, and seal in a polythene bag. Leave the 3 cakes overnight.

to build the cake

Spread 1–2 tbsp royal icing into the centre of the base drum. Gently ease away the largest cake and drum from its board using a palette knife and place it exactly in the middle of the base drum.

Now insert 4 dowelling sticks into the large cake, spacing them to form the corners of a square just within where the 20cm cake will sit. Push down each stick until it hits the drum, and mark with a pen about 1mm proud of the surface. Remove each stick, score with a knife at the mark, snap and discard the excess. Replace each in its hole.

Spread a spoonful of royal icing into the centre of the largest cake, remove the 20cm cake and drum from its thin board and place centrally on top of the larger cake, resting the drum on the hidden dowels. Repeat the dowel placing process with this middle tier to add the top cake, again using a spoonful of royal icing to keep it steady.

FOR THE CONSTRUCTION
1 x 30cm diameter, 1cm thick, square cake drum
8 dowelling sticks

FOR COVERING THE CAKES
icing sugar, to dust
4kg ready mixed 'Celebration' cream-coloured sugarpaste
2 tbsp brandy or boiled water
8–10 tbsp white royal icing

decoration

to make the butterflies and blossoms

You will need about 12–15 butterflies and about 100 blossoms in 3 sizes (I made 25 tiny 5mm blossoms, 25 medium 10mm blossoms and 50 large 15mm blossoms).

The decorations are applied randomly, so this is just a guide. Knead some of the sugarpaste left over from covering the cakes and drums until pliable, and roll out thinly (to 2mm thick) on a board dusted with a little icing sugar. Stamp out the blossoms and butterflies and allow to dry for a few hours, or preferably overnight. I lay them out as I make them in boxes interleaved with silicone paper. Prop up the butterflies' wings between two sticks (you could use spare dowelling rods), so the wings will dry as if in flight.

If you like, pipe the centres of the blossoms with a tiny dot of royal icing and then press on a gold dragee. If you prefer, just pipe a dot for the centres. Once the butterflies are dry, paint the edges of the wings with egg white and dip into the glitter.

To finish the cake, apply the ribbons by sticking them at the back of each cake using a little royal icing. On the middle tier, overlay the wide organza ribbon with 2 bands of narrow gold ribbon. Wrap the base drum with the double-sided sticky tape, then stick on its ribbon.

Casual, informal designs do have one huge advantage: any blemishes or marks in the icing can be covered by a decoration! Randomly apply the butterflies and little blossoms all over the 3-tiered cake, sticking on with the royal icing. As a final touch, place the 2 doves in the centre of the top tier.

FOR THE ADORNMENTS

icing sugar, to dust
set of 3 blossom cutters
    (5mm, 10mm, 15mm)
30mm butterfly cutter
30g bag white royal icing
100 small gold dragees in 2 sizes
    (optional); I used 50 medium
    and 50 small gold dragees
1 small paint brush
1 egg white, lightly beaten
1 pot edible gold glitter
2 small artificial cream or white
    doves (or other birds)

FOR THE TOP TIER
75cm 3.5cm-wide vintage
    gold ribbon

FOR THE MIDDLE TIER
95cm 4cm-wide cream organza
190cm 3mm-wide gold ribbon

FOR THE BOTTOM TIER
120cm 5.5cm-wide gold
    bejewelled ribbon

FOR THE BASE DRUM
1 roll double-sided sticky tape,
    12mm wide
130cm-plus 1.5cm-wide cream
    ribbon

TO BAKE see: Rich Tamarind Fruit Cake, p46

chocolate spiral

I love this unusual cone-shaped cake. I know someone who
once used a traffic cone to make it... not to be encouraged!
It is very easy, though fairly messy. Try to make this in the
cooler months, when working with chocolate and making
chocolate leaves is so much easier.

Make the cone. The centre of the long side of the cardboard is to be
its tip. Twist the cardboard around, tape very firmly into place and
cut the base flat; your cone should be about 35cm high and 20cm in
diameter. Very lightly butter the inside and line with clingfilm. Stand
it upside down in a suitable stable container, such as a large vase.

Now cut out rounds of cake with a sharp knife, using cutters, mugs,
saucers or small tins as guides. Place the smallest disc in the tip of
the mould, then spread with icing. Layer in more discs, getting ever
bigger and spreading icing in between. Fill in gaps with pieces of cake
and finish with an entire cake as the base. Refrigerate overnight to set.

Carefully invert the cone on to its final serving plate or stand. Remove
the cardboard and clingfilm. Make a tip with the sugarpaste or
marzipan and, with a little icing, stick it on top. Spread the remaining
icing all around the cake, filling in gaps and smoothing the sides.

To make the chocolate leaves, place a small heatproof bowl over a
saucepan of gently simmering water, making sure the base
of the bowl does not touch the water. Add the chocolate
and heat until melted, stirring only very occasionally.
Dip the undersides of the leaves into the chocolate. Place,
chocolate-side up, on a tray lined with baking parchment,
propped up on bits of rolled-up foil so they don't lie
completely flat. When the chocolate has hardened (give it
a spell in the refrigerator), gently peel off the real leaves,
holding the stems. You may break a few (I do!) so make
more than you need. (I used 60 on the cake.) Stick the
leaves on to the iced cone in a spiral. Overlap the leaves
and, if any edges are slightly broken, hide them behind
another overlapping leaf. Finish with the gold dragees.

TO BAKE see: Family Chocolate Cake, p17

SERVES 25–30

2 x Family Chocolate Cake
    (see p17)
2 x recipe Fudge Icing (see p17)

1 x A1 sheet cardboard
strong sticky tape
butter, for the mould
40g sugarpaste or marzipan
100g 70% cocoa solids
    chocolate, broken into squares
60–70 mint or rose leaves with
    prominent veins, washed and
    dried thoroughly
60 gold dragees

tiered marie antoinette's cake

Whether she did or didn't actually say 'let them eat cake', I choose to think that she did! Inspired by the exquisite costumes and dazzling confections of the French court at the Palace of Versailles, this beautiful cake is fit for a queen, with its adornments of ostrich feathers, pearls, ribbons and rosebuds. Ideal for a wedding or special birthday party.

MAKES 80 SMALL PIECES

the nuts and bolts

You can both make and freeze the unadorned cakes and prepare the lavender sugar a month in advance if you want to get ahead. Thin cake boards are only to assemble the cakes, so use any board you have. Cake drums support each tier, so must be bought for the purpose.

You need to make 3 cakes, as the 2 larger cakes, sandwiched together, form the bottom tier. Follow the instructions for making the Orange Drizzle Cake (see p32), baking the 1 smaller, deeper cake for 40–45 minutes and the 2 larger, shallower cakes for just 35–40 minutes.

Tip the icing sugar into a food processor and add the lavender. Process until very fine, then store in a sealed container for a week to allow the flavour to develop. Sift and store in a dry, airtight container.

to buttercream the cakes
In an electric mixer, cream the butter and lemon zest for 1–2 minutes until fluffy, then add half the sugar. Mix for 5 minutes, then add the remaining sugar and the juice and mix for 1–2 minutes. Trim the tops of all 3 cakes with a serrated knife just until level. The cakes should be about the same height once filled, so fill the smaller cake with more buttercream than the larger, and fill in any holes or cracks as well.

Slice the smaller cake in half and place the top half upside down on to its 20cm drum, securing with a little buttercream. Place this on the smaller thin board. Spread buttercream on the cut surface, then top with the other half. The flat base now forms the top. For the larger cake, place 1 cake on the 25cm cake drum, again securing with buttercream, and lift on to the 30cm thin board. Spread buttercream on, then top with the second cake, inverted so its base forms the top. Smooth the remaining buttercream over the top and sides of both.

FOR THE CAKES
1 x 20cm diameter, 7.5cm deep, round tin
2 x 25cm diameter, 7.5cm deep, round tins
3 x Orange Drizzle Cake batter (see p32), with the orange zest and juice replaced by lemon zest and juice

FOR THE LAVENDER SUGAR
550g icing sugar, sifted
12 dry, unsprayed lavender flower heads, in full bloom

FOR THE BUTTERCREAM
450g unsalted butter, softened
zest of 2 unwaxed lemons, finely grated
550g lavender icing sugar, sifted
juice of 1 lemon

FOR THE BOARDS AND DRUMS
1 x 20cm diameter, 1cm thick, round cake drum
1 x 25cm diameter, 1cm thick, round cake drum
1 x 30cm diameter, 1cm thick, round cake drum
1 x 25cm round thin board
1 x 30cm round thin board

assembly

to colour the sugarpaste

Cut off 100g of the sugarpaste and place it in a sealed polythene bag at room temperature. This will make the roses and rosebuds. Colour the remaining sugarpaste with the food colour paste (see p11), aiming for the pale pink shown overleaf. Divide into 3 - 1 part for the base drum and 1 part for each cake - place into separate polythene food bags and seal. Rest it overnight at room temperature.

to cover the base drum

Dust the 30cm drum with icing sugar and sprinkle with water. Knead a third of the pink sugarpaste until pliable, then, on a surface lightly dusted with icing sugar, roll out into a circle slightly larger than the top of the drum and about 3mm thick. Wrap it loosely around the rolling pin and lift on to the drum. Smooth with your hands. Trim away any excess overhanging the sides and reseal it in the bag. Leave at room temperature overnight before decorating.

to cover the cakes

Lightly dust a clean, flat surface with icing sugar. Roll out both the remaining pink sugarpaste blocks, one at a time, into circles about 5mm thick and slightly larger than the diameter of each cake, its sides and drum. Wrap each circle loosely around the rolling pin, place it over the cake and gently smooth with your hands. Do not stretch the sugarpaste, and work quickly, as it will dry out. Cut away any excess at the foot of the drums and reseal it in the bag. Take a large knife and roll it gently along the top surface of the cakes, scoring lines to form a criss-cross (each line about 1½cm apart) to resemble quilting. Push a dragee in where the lines meet. The centre of the bottom tier will not be seen, so no need to use dragees. Leave overnight.

to build the cake

Spread 3-4 tbsp of royal icing into the centre of the base drum. Ease the larger cake and drum from its thin board with a palette knife, and place it in the exact centre of the base drum. Now insert the dowelling sticks vertically into the cake, spacing them out to form the corners of a square just within where the smaller cake will sit. Push down each stick until it hits the drum, and mark with a pen about 1mm proud of the surface. Remove each stick, score with a knife at the mark, then snap and discard the excess. Replace each in its hole. Spread 3-4 tbsp royal icing into the centre of the larger cake, remove the smaller cake and drum from its thin board and place on top, resting the drum on the dowels and using the royal icing as 'glue'.

FOR THE SUGARPASTE
3kg white sugarpaste
1 pot Sugarflair Claret
   food colour paste

FOR THE CONSTRUCTION
icing sugar, to dust
200 silver dragees
6–8 tbsp white royal icing
4 dowelling sticks

decoration

No cutters are required for this cake and, if piping swags seems too difficult, just pipe simple dots around the edges. Fresh flowers could be used on top instead of the sugarpaste roses, if you prefer. You should find a good supply of beading, braids and feathers in a haberdashery department.

to make the roses and rosebuds

Turn to the reserved white sugarpaste. Tint about 40g of it green and 60g off-white, using a tiny amount of Eucalyptus and a pinprick of Caramel/Ivory pastes respectively (see p11). Tint about 300g of the pink sugarpaste reserved from covering the cake a deeper pink, using more Claret paste. Reseal all colours in separate polythene bags.

Make a few rosebuds at a time. On a board dusted with icing sugar, roll out a little deeper pink sugarpaste to 1mm thick. Cut into strips of 10cm x 1 ½cm and roll each into little buds. Cut away surplus at the base. Repeat to make 16. Make the leaves with the green sugarpaste. Take a little ball at a time and shape into a tiny leaf. Score with a knife to resemble the central vein. Make 3 large (4cm) leaves and pinch to make the veins. Dip into glitter. Allow all rosebuds and leaves to dry, preferably overnight.

To make the larger roses, see p129, forming one each from ivory, lighter and deeper pink sugarpaste. When dry, paint the edges of the petals with egg white, dip into the glitter, then shake off excess.

the finishing touches

Apply all the ribbons, braids and beading by sticking them at the back of the cake using a little royal icing. Use the double-sided tape to stick the braid to the side of the base drum. Stick on the rosebuds and leaves with royal icing, spacing them out at 7cm apart on the top tier and 10cm apart on the bottom tier. Each tier will have 8 rosebuds.

Push the flower pick into the centre of the cake. Stand the ostrich feather and pearl spray in this, using a little sugarpaste inside the tube to support it if necessary. Use the royal icing to adhere the 3 large roses and leaves around the base of the feather.

Finish the cake by piping half-circle swags between the rosebuds, then dots. This is easier if you gently tilt the cake up towards you by placing a book under the board. Simple tiny randomly piped dots, about 25mm apart, all over the sides will look just as effective.

TO BAKE see: Orange Drizzle Cake, p32

FOR THE ROSES AND ROSEBUDS
1 pot Sugarflair Eucalyptus food colour paste
1 pot Sugarflair Caramel/Ivory food colour paste
1 egg white
1 pot clear edible glitter
70g bag white royal icing, No. 1 nozzle

FOR THE BASE DRUM
100cm braid or ribbon, 1.5cm wide
1 roll of double-sided sticky tape, 12mm wide

FOR THE BOTTOM TIER
90cm pale pink satin ribbon
90cm thinner braided ribbon, ideally in pink and pale green

FOR THE TOP TIER
70cm pale cream and pink ribbon
70cm pearl beading
1 flower pick, or small plastic tube from a florist
1 ostrich feather
1 spray of pearls on wires

small cakes

butterfly cakes

Quintessentially British and universally popular.

Preheat the oven to 180°C/fan 170°C/350°F/gas mark 4.

Place the paper cases into 2 fairy cake tins and divide the batter evenly between them. Bake for about 15 minutes, or until the cakes are well risen and spring back to the touch. Leave in the tins for 1–2 minutes, then remove to cool completely on a wire rack.

For the vanilla buttercream, cream the butter until pale and fluffy, add the vanilla and then the icing sugar. Beat for about 5 minutes until really light. Make the chocolate buttercream in the same way, adding the cocoa powder with the icing sugar and omitting the vanilla.

To make the wings, cut out a shallow dome from the top of each cake and cut the slice in half. Spoon a swirl of buttercream into the cut-out dip on top of each cake and place the wings back in at an angle. Dust with icing sugar and arrange on a cake stand or plate.

MAKES 18–20 FAIRY CAKES

1 x Victoria Sponge batter
  (see p24)

18–20 fairy cake cases
icing sugar, to dust

FOR VANILLA BUTTERCREAM
200g unsalted butter, softened
1 tsp vanilla extract
250g icing sugar, sifted

FOR CHOCOLATE BUTTERCREAM
200g unsalted butter, softened
50g cocoa powder
200g icing sugar, sifted

TO BAKE see: Victoria Sponge, p24

garland cakes

These exquisitely intricate paper collars wrap around the cupcakes, which are very simply iced and decorated. You can create an impressive display with very little effort and you should be able to reuse the collars. I used a brand called Paper Orchid, which comes in packs of 12 (see suppliers, p207). I added 1½ tsp of very tiny dragees for this photo, but you can use all the same size if it's easier.

Preheat the oven to 180°C/fan 170°C/350°F/gas mark 4.

Place the cases into a cupcake tin and divide the batter evenly between them. Bake for 15–20 minutes, or until the cakes are well risen and spring back to the touch. Leave to cool in the tins for 1–2 minutes, then remove to cool on a wire rack.

Make the topping by creaming the butter, sugar and zest for about 5 minutes until pale and fluffy, then add the mascarpone, vanilla and Cointreau (do not over-mix as it may become too liquid). Pipe the buttercream on to each cake using the star nozzle and piping bag. Sprinkle the silver dragees on to the cakes in silver cases, and the gold dragees on to the cakes in gold cases.

When ready to serve, make up the 12 paper collars, place a cake in each one and display.

MAKES 12 CUPCAKES

1 x Victoria Sponge batter
  (see p24)

6 silver cupcake cases
6 gold cupcake cases
100g unsalted butter, softened
100g icing sugar
zest of 2 oranges, finely grated
500g mascarpone
1 tsp vanilla extract
1 tbsp Cointreau (optional)
large star nozzle
nylon piping bag
3 tsp silver and gold dragees
12 cupcake collars

TO BAKE see: Victoria Sponge, p24

rosebud fairy cakes

A cake stand piled with these enchanting creations in pastel pinks would be lovely for a girlie afternoon tea or birthday party. Make more for a larger celebration or even a wedding. The rosebuds can be made a month or 2 in advance; store in a cardboard box at room temperature.

Preheat the oven to 180°C/fan 170°C/350°F/gas mark 4. Place the cases into 2 fairy cake tins and divide the batter evenly between them. Bake for about 15 minutes or until well risen and the cakes spring back to the touch. Leave to cool in the tins for 1–2 minutes, then remove to cool on a wire rack.

Make the buttercream. Cream the butter until pale and fluffy, add the rosewater, if liked, and the vanilla, then beat in the icing sugar for about 5 minutes until really light, adding enough food colour paste to achieve the shade of pink you want. Divide between all the cakes, spreading with a palette knife.

To make the rosebuds, divide the sugarpaste into 3 and colour each a different shade of pink (start with the darkest pink, see p11). Seal in separate polythene bags. On a board lightly dusted with icing sugar, and with a dusted rolling pin, roll out a little of the sugarpaste to about 1–2mm thick. Cut 3 or 4 strips about 10x1 ½ cm and roll them up to form rosebuds. Cut away any surplus at the base. Repeat until you have made 24 buds, 8 in each tone of pink. Place 1 on each cake.

Snip the green royal icing bag in a V-shape (the 'V' should point towards the bag) and use it to pipe a leaf or 2 on each cake, or leave some without if you prefer. Scatter glitter over the cakes, if you wish.

MAKES 24 FAIRY CAKES

1 x Victoria Sponge batter
   (see p24)

24 fairy cake cases
200g butter, softened
1 tsp rosewater (optional)
1 tsp vanilla extract
250g icing sugar, plus more
   to dust
1 pot pink food colour paste
150g white sugarpaste
60g bag green royal icing
1 pot clear glitter (optional)

TO BAKE see: Victoria Sponge, p24

crystallised flower fairy cakes

Perfect for any garden party, these are as pretty as a picture. In this recipe, they are iced in very pale lavender and green pastels to complement the flowers used, but you can use any colours of your choice. For a large party or wedding, a stand of these on each table would make a fabulous centrepiece.

Preheat the oven to 170ºC/fan 160ºC/340ºF/gas mark 3½.

Line 2 fairy cake tins with paper cases. Divide the batter evenly between them (make sure each is only just over half full, as you need space for the icing to set flat on top). Bake for 15 minutes, or until the cakes are well risen and spring back to the touch. Leave for 1–2 minutes in the tins, then place on a wire rack until cold.

Divide the icing sugar between 2 bowls. Very gradually add a little orange juice to each until it is thick enough to coat the back of a spoon. Add a very little purple food colour to 1 bowl and blend it in well until you achieve the desired shade. Cover the bowl with clingfilm (the icing dries out very quickly) while you colour the other bowl in the same way, using the green food colour.

To ice the cakes, replace them in the fairy cake tins. This makes it much easier as the tins will hold the shapes of the cakes. Spread enough icing on to the cakes - using each colour on about half the batch - so that it is almost level with the top of the case, gently easing it to the edges with the back of a spoon. Allow to dry for a couple of hours. The cakes can be iced 2 days ahead, but add the flowers on the day they are to be eaten.

To finish, arrange the crystallised flowers and leaves on the cakes, using dabs of royal icing to hold them in place. Display on cake stands or plates, scattering any remaining flowers and leaves in between.

MAKES 20–24

1 x Orange Drizzle Cake batter (see p32)

20–24 fairy cake cases
600g icing sugar, sifted
5–7 tbsp orange juice
purple food colour
green food colour
20–30 edible crystallised flowers and leaves (I used lavender, tiny rosebuds, anchusa, daisies and pinks, and geranium and rosemary leaves, see p107)
70g bag white royal icing

TO BAKE see: Orange Drizzle Cake, p32

ice-cream cones

Ice-creams that won't melt! A perfect addition to any children's party or picnic, especially during the summer. These are decorated as the real things - flake 99, raspberry ripple or mint choc chip - but use your imagination and get the children to give you a hand. These cakes are baked in ice-cream cones, so eat them quickly as they will start to dry out after a day or so. That shouldn't prove difficult!

Preheat the oven to 170ºC/fan 160ºC/340ºF/gas mark 3½. Place all the ice-cream cones on a baking sheet. Divide the cake batter evenly between them and bake for 15–17 minutes, or until they spring back to the touch. Leave to cool on a wire rack.

Divide the buttercream between 3 bowls. Add a little peppermint extract to the first, to taste, then a dash of green food colour, and mix until you achieve the desired shade. Add the vanilla to the second bowl and mix well. To the third bowl, swirl in a little pink food colour; do not blend it in as you are aiming for the marbled effect of raspberry ripple ice-cream.

Spoon the vanilla buttercream into the piping bag and swirl on to a third of the ice-cream cones. Finish each with a chocolate flake. Wash the bag and nozzle and repeat with the green buttercream; sprinkling with chocolate buttons. Wash the bag and nozzle again. Finally pipe the raspberry ripple buttercream into the remaining cones and decorate with sprinkles.

Arrange on a serving dish or cake stand.

MAKES 20–25

1 x Orange Drizzle Cake batter
(see p32)

20–25 flat-based ice-cream cones
1 x recipe Buttercream (see p9)
few drops of peppermint extract
green food colour
1 tsp vanilla extract
pink (or red) food colour
nylon piping bag
large star nozzle
7–8 chocolate flakes
7 tsp tiny chocolate buttons
5 tsp coloured sugar sprinkles

TO BAKE see: Orange Drizzle Cake, p32

fondant fancies

From a very young age, the cakes my children wanted to eat were fondant fancies in pastel colours, found on every supermarket shelf. Every cake I made was up for comparison and rarely equalled them; never surpassing! Here are my fondant fancies with a contemporary twist, iced in 4 colours. You could easily use fewer colours; choose whichever appeal to you.

Preheat the oven to 180ºC/fan 170ºC/350ºF/gas mark 4. Butter a 20cm diameter, 7cm deep, square tin and line with baking parchment. Fill the tin with the batter and bake for about 35 minutes, or until a skewer inserted into the centre of the cake comes out clean. Leave for a few minutes, then turn out on to a wire rack until cold.

Make the buttercream using the butter, 110g of the icing sugar and the vanilla (see p9). Split the cake horizontally, fill with buttercream and place in the refrigerator or freezer to firm up for about 1 hour.

Meanwhile prepare the glacé icing. Place the remaining icing sugar into a large bowl and gradually add water until the icing is thick enough to coat the back of a spoon. Keep it fairly stiff, as the food colours will make the icing runnier.

Divide into 4 bowls. Blend Claret food colour paste into the first to make a pale pink; Eucalyptus, Ice Blue and Primrose to another for the green; Primrose and a pin prick of Claret to the third for yellow; Grape Violet and a little Claret to the last for purple. Cover all the bowls with clingfilm so the icing doesn't dry out.

Take the cake out of the refrigerator or freezer and, with a sharp knife, cut into 25 little squares. Turn each upside down so its flat base forms the top surface. Take 6 and place on a wire rack. Spoon over 1 colour of the glacé icing, easing it down the sides with the back of a teaspoon. While still wet, decorate with your chosen decorations: tiny sugar flowers, dragees, or angelica. Use leftover glacé icing in a contrasting colour to decorate: place a little into a piping bag, snip the end and pipe in a zigzag fashion over the top of some of the cakes. Repeat with another 6 cakes and another colour, until all are iced.

TO BAKE see: Victoria Sponge, p24

MAKES 25

1 x Victoria Sponge batter (see p24)

90g unsalted butter, softened, plus more for the tin
1.36kg icing sugar, sifted
1 tsp vanilla extract
1 pot Sugarflair Claret food colour paste
1 pot Sugarflair Eucalyptus food colour paste
1 pot Sugarflair Ice-blue food colour paste
1 pot Sugarflair Primrose food colour paste
1 pot Sugarflair Grape Violet food colour paste
selection of tiny sugar flowers, dragees and angelica
2 small piping bags

mint cupcakes

I love the contrast between chocolate cake and this pale mint buttercream. Be careful, when buying the chocolate, to avoid a bar with a fondant centre! Naturally, the chocolate itself should contain the mint flavour.

Preheat the oven to 180°C/fan 170°C/350°F/gas mark 4.

Place the paper cases into a cupcake tin and divide the batter between them. Bake for 25–30 minutes. When they spring back to the touch, remove to cool on a wire rack.

Meanwhile, beat together the butter and icing sugar for a good 5 minutes until really light, then add the peppermint extract and a touch of green food colour paste.

With a palette knife, spread buttercream on to the cupcakes and decorate each with a sprig of mint.

MAKES 16–18

1 x Family Chocolate Cake batter, made with mint dark chocolate (see p17)

18 cupcake cases
200g unsalted butter, softened
250g icing sugar, sifted
few drops of peppermint extract, to taste
1 pot green food colour paste
18 sprigs fresh or crystallised mint leaves (see p107)

TO BAKE see: Family Chocolate Cake, p17

chilli chocolate cupcakes

Chilli-flavoured chocolate is used for this lovely, shiny icing and each cake is decorated with a whole chilli... munch on it at your peril! Don't worry about the heat of the chocolate icing itself, though, as it only has a mild kick. I also give recipes for a chocolate-vanilla and a chocolate-mocha icing here, in case chillies aren't for you.

Preheat the oven to 170°C/fan 160°C/340°F/gas mark 3½. Place the cupcake cases into 2 x 12-hole cupcake tins. Divide the batter evenly between them and bake for 17–20 minutes, or until the cakes spring back to the touch. Don't worry if they crack in the oven; the icing will cover any fissures. Remove and cool on a wire rack.

Meanwhile, make the icing. In a heavy-based pan, gently heat together 125ml water, the sugar, chocolate and syrup and bring to the boil, stirring so it doesn't catch on the bottom of the pan. Stir constantly for about 3 minutes, or until thickened. Remove from the heat and stir in the butter.

Allow to cool, then spoon over the cupcakes. If the icing becomes too thick before you have finished coating the cakes, simply reheat it very gently. Place a chilli on each cake as you apply the icing, then leave to cool completely and set.

icing flavourings

chocolate-vanilla use unflavoured dark chocolate and add 1 tsp vanilla extract with the butter

chocolate-mocha use unflavoured dark chocolate and replace the 125ml water with strong coffee.

MAKES 15

½ x recipe Chocolate Celebration
   Cake batter (see p14)

15 cupcake cases
65g white caster sugar
160g 55–70% cocoa solids
   chilli-flavoured chocolate,
   finely chopped
2 tbsp golden syrup
30g unsalted butter
15 red chillies

TO BAKE see: Chocolate Celebration Cake, p14

daisy and sunflower cupcakes

The vogue for cupcakes started in New York. I took a trip there recently, and was fascinated by all the vibrant colours. These are inspired by those Manhattan creations.

Preheat the oven to 160ºC/fan 150ºC/325ºF/gas mark 3.

Place the paper cases into a cupcake tin. Divide the batter between them and bake for 25–30 minutes or until they spring back to the touch. Leave in the tin for a minute or 2, then cool on a wire rack.

Meanwhile make the topping. Beat the butter, icing sugar, zest and maple syrup until really light and fluffy. In a separate bowl beat the cream cheese until smooth, then fold into the butter mixture; do not over-mix as it may become too runny to pipe. If it is too soft, chill for an hour to firm it up. Divide into 2 bowls and colour the first a pale sunflower yellow, adding more icing sugar if it becomes too liquid.

Fill 1 piping bag with yellow icing and the other with plain. Snip a V shape into each end (with the point of the 'V' facing the bag) and pipe petals on to each cake. Pipe a little icing into the centre and fill with mini beans; yellow for daisies and brown for sunflowers.

MAKES 12

1 x Carrot-Pecan Cake batter
  (see p43)

12 cupcake cases
80g unsalted butter
60g icing sugar, sifted
zest of 1 orange, finely grated
1 tbsp maple syrup
150g cream cheese
yellow food colour paste
2 piping bags
96 yellow mini chocolate beans
96 brown mini chocolate beans

TO BAKE see: Carrot-Pecan Cake, p43

parcels

We all love to receive a beautifully wrapped gift and these edible parcels are a delight. Children will love to decorate them, too, and the possibilities are endless (see p202). You could decorate a large cake instead of quarters, if you prefer.

Preheat the oven to 180°C/fan 170°C/350°F/gas mark 4. Butter a 23cm square tin and line the base with baking parchment. Fill with the batter and bake for 40–50 minutes, or until a skewer inserted into the centre comes out clean. Leave until completely cold.

Place the cake in the refrigerator for an hour or 2. It will be firmer and, therefore, less crumbly when you cut it. Turn it upside down, split it and sandwich with some of the fudge icing. Trim the sides, then cut the cake into 4 equal squares. Place on the boards, adhering with a dab of fudge icing in the middle. Spread a little fudge icing over the top and sides of each. Great care needs to be taken here not to spread it right down to the board; stop about 1cm above it otherwise the fudge icing will soil the white sugarpaste.

Separate the sugarpaste into 4 portions. Dust a work top and your rolling pin with a little icing sugar, then roll out 1 piece at a time to a square about 5mm thick and slightly larger than the top and sides of the cake. Lift on to a cake, smooth with your hands, then cut away the excess. Repeat with the other 3 cakes.

Make 'paper folds' with the blunt side of a knife on 2 opposite ends of each parcel. Secure a piece of ribbon at the opposite bases of each parcel using royal icing and repeat with another ribbon. Do not tuck the ribbons under the cake or they may become stained. Tie a ribbon bow and stick it, with a tassel, in the centre of each parcel. Finally, decorate the 'wrapping paper' by sticking on the mini beans.

MAKES 4

1 x Family Chocolate Cake batter (see p17)
1 x recipe Fudge Icing (see p17)

butter, for the tin
4 x 15cm square, thin cake boards
1.2kg white sugarpaste
icing sugar, to dust
4 x 80cm long, 15mm-wide ribbons in contrasting colours
60g bag white royal icing
4 tassels
80 mini chocolate beans in 4 colours

TO BAKE see: Family Chocolate Cake, p17

fancy hats

Become a milliner and design your own hats in cake and icing. I have created a smart black-and-white hat fit for a race meeting or any wedding, a top hat, a cap, a trilby and summer boaters. Take these as a starting point and create your own range of exquisite headgear!

Colour 100g of sugarpaste for the top hat, using the black and violet food pastes (see p11) and seal in a polythene bag. Cut 1 of the 7.5cm cake boards down to 5cm diameter (you can't buy 5cm cake boards!).

Dust all the cake boards with a little icing sugar and sprinkle with water. Make the rims of the hats: on a work top lightly dusted with icing sugar, and with a dusted rolling pin, roll out some of the white sugarpaste to 3mm thick. Using the round cutters, cut out 2 x 10cm rounds, 3 x 7.5cm rounds and 1 x 5cm round. Place these on their appropriate boards. Roll out a little of the coloured sugarpaste to the same thickness, cut out 1 x 7.5cm round and place on the remaining cake board. Spread a little jam into the centre of each board.

Now take the cutters to the Victoria Sponge. These circles of cake will form the hat crowns. Using more of the jam, sandwich together 2 x 5cm rounds for the top hat, 3 x 5cm rounds for the race meeting hat and 2 x 4cm rounds for the cap. Cut the top layer of the cap at an angle, with a sharp knife, so the crown slopes backwards. Cut out 4 more 5cm rounds for the remaining cakes. Brush each with jam.

Next, dusting the work surface and rolling pin with a little icing sugar, roll out the remaining white sugarpaste and use it to cover each cake crown (except for the top hat). Cover the top hat with the coloured sugarpaste. Smooth with your hands and, when you are pleased with the shapes, put the cakes on their boards, placing the cap towards the rear of the smallest cake board to make a 'peak'. Run a finger down the centre of the trilby to indent. Leave to dry overnight.

To decorate the hats, use royal icing to attach the ribbons, netting, dragees, feathers, braid and silk flowers, as you wish.

TO BAKE see: Victoria Sponge, p24

MAKES 7 HATS

1 x 20cm Victoria Sponge baked in 2 sandwich tins (see p24)

700g white sugarpaste
1 pot black food colour paste
1 pot violet food colour paste
5 x 7.5cm thin round cake boards
2 x 10cm thin round cake boards
icing sugar, to dust
1 x set round metal cutters (10cm, 7.5cm, 5cm and 4cm)
8 tbsp apricot jam, warmed and sieved
60g bag white royal icing
selection of ribbons, netting, dragees, feathers, braid and tiny silk flowers

mini tiered cakes

A recipe made in cupcake, fairy cake and tiny petit four cases and stacked up high; tiered cakes don't need to be kept for weddings! This recipe is very versatile: try it with Family Chocolate Cake (p17); Victoria Sponge (p24); Very Lemony Crunch Cake (p31) or Orange Drizzle Cake (p32).

Colour the sugarpaste using a very little of the food colour paste (see p11). Seal in a polythene bag at room temperature until ready to use.

Preheat the oven to 160°C/fan 150°C/325°F/gas mark 3. Place the fairy cake and cupcake cases in the appropriate baking tins, and the petit four cases in a small holed baking tray if you have one (if you don't, just place them on a baking sheet, though be prepared for them to be a little irregular in shape). Pour in the batter. Bake the tinies for approximately 15 minutes, the middle-sized for 20 minutes and the largest for 25–30 minutes, or until each springs back to the touch.

Remove from the oven and cool on a wire rack. When cold, take each cake out of its paper case. Warm the apricot jam in a small pan, sieve and brush all over the top surfaces of the cakes. Roll out the sugarpaste on a work surface lightly dusted with icing sugar (dust your rolling pin too) to around 5mm thick. Cut out 8 discs in each of the 3 sizes and place on top of the cakes. Place a dab of royal icing on a cupcake, put a fairy cake on top, add another dab of royal icing and top with a tiny cake. Repeat until you have made all 8 cakes.

Decorate with 8 dragees on the top tier, 6 little sugar flowers around the middle tier and about 8 on the bottom, using the royal icing to adhere. Cut 8 x 20cm strips of the thinnest ribbon for the top tier and simply cross over at the front, adhering with a little royal icing at the back. Repeat with the middle and bottom layers using roughly 30cm strips of the contrasting 5mm-wide and 24mm-wide ribbon respectively. These cakes can be stored in an airtight container for up to 2 days; no longer, as they will dry out more quickly than usual because their paper cases have been removed.

TO BAKE see: Carrot-Pecan Cake, p43

MAKES 8 CAKES

1 x Carrot-Pecan Cake batter (see p43)

400g white sugarpaste
1 pot violet food colour paste
8 fairy cake cases
8 cupcake cases
8 petit four cases
3 tbsp apricot jam
icing sugar, to dust
3 sizes fluted round cutters, (I used 33mm, 50mm, 65mm)
60g bag white royal icing
64 coloured dragees
112 tiny sugar flowers
160cm 5mm-wide ribbon
240cm 5mm-wide contrasting ribbon
240cm 24mm-wide ribbon

flying insects

Flying insects and wriggly worms will delight young children, both to make and to eat (especially the worms). The insects can be made a few weeks ahead, and must be finished at least the day before, and stored in a cardboard box at room temperature.

Make all the insects at least the day before. Divide the sugarpaste into 5 bowls. Colour them red, pink, black and yellow (see p11). Leave the last one white. Seal in 5 polythene bags at room temperature.

For the ladybirds, roll 8 red balls and shape them to be narrower towards the head. With a knife, make a seam down the middle for the wings. Make a little ball of black and, with black royal icing, attach these heads to the bodies. Pipe 2 eyes with white royal icing, then black dots on to the back. To make the spiders, roll the remaining black sugarpaste into 8 balls, flatten and roll in chocolate sprinkles. For the legs, cut 4 x 5cm liquorice strands per spider and attach to the underside with black royal icing. Pipe 2 eyes in white.

For the worms, roll 8 sausages of pink sugarpaste - wider at one end for the head - and indent with the knife along the backs. Make the tails by rolling 8 smaller sausages and indent again. Pipe 2 white eyes. To make the bees, shape 8 yellow balls, making the head end a little wider, and pipe 3 black stripes over each body and 2 black eyes. Roll the white sugarpaste out and cut out 16 hearts (or mould 16 ovals) to form wings. Attach with white royal icing.

Preheat the oven to 180°C/fan 170°C/350°F/gas mark 4. Place the paper cases into 3 fairy cake tins (or bake in batches). Pour in the batter and bake for 12–15 minutes. Remove from the oven, stand for a couple of minutes, then cool on a wire rack. Ice with the buttercream.

Push a cocktail stick into each insect. Attach 1 insect to each cake; for the worms, make 2 holes with the end of a teaspoon and push a head and a tail into 8 cakes so the worm seems to be crawling through. Scatter ¼ tsp sprinkles on the spider and worm cakes. Arrange 5 red mini beans around the base of each ladybird and 5 pink for the bees.

TO BAKE see: Sticky Toffee Cupcakes, p64

MAKES 32 FAIRY CAKES

1 x Sticky Toffee Cupcakes batter (see p64)

350g white sugarpaste
red food colour paste
pink food colour paste
black food colour paste
yellow food colour paste
50g bag black royal icing
50g bag white royal icing
4 tsp chocolate sprinkles
8 long black liquorice strands
icing sugar, to dust
1 x 15mm heart cutter (optional)
32 fairy cake cases
1 x recipe vanilla Buttercream (see p9)
24 cocktail sticks
2 tsp coloured sprinkles
40 red mini chocolate beans
40 pink mini chocolate beans

fairy tale garden cakes

Create an enchanting flower garden just like a child's drawing; perfect for a birthday party. Lollipop 'flowers', green sugar 'grass' and angelica 'leaves' mean these little orange and lemon cakes take no time at all.

Make the 'grass' by mixing a drop or two of water and the green food colour together in a small bowl, then add the sugar. Rub together with your fingers until all the sugar has been dyed. Allow to dry for a few hours. Preheat the oven to 180ºC/fan 170ºC/350ºF/gas mark 4.

Place the paper cases into 2 fairy cake trays, divide the batter between them and bake for 20–25 minutes, or until they spring back to the touch. Cool on a wire rack.

When the cakes are cold, spread the buttercream over the surface of each cake. Sprinkle over the coloured sugar.

Soften the angelica for a minute or so in warm water. Make the leaves by snipping the angelica into narrow strips and then diagonally across into diamonds. Place a lollipop 'flower' into the centre of each cake and surround with 2 angelica 'leaves'. Arrange on a cake stand or serving plate, or even under a cloche or among a few flower pots.

MAKES 15

1 x Very Lemony Crunch Cake batter (see p31)

green food colour
60g granulated sugar
15 fairy cake cases
½ x recipe orange Buttercream (see p9)
50g tub crystallised angelica
15 lollipops

TO BAKE see: Very Lemony Crunch Cake, p31

tiny fairy cakes

These dinky little bite-sized cakes are made in petit four cases. The blossoms and butterflies can be made ahead and stored at room temperature in a cardboard box, not in an airtight container or sealed tin. The cakes themselves can be made 2 days ahead, but no longer or they will dry out.

Preheat the oven to 180°C/fan 170°C/350°F/gas mark 4. Lay out all the petit four cases in small-hole baking trays, or just put them on baking sheets. Divide the batter evenly between them and bake for 8–10 minutes, or until the cakes spring back to the touch. Cool on a wire rack. The shapes may be irregular but that is part of their charm.

Place the icing sugar into a bowl and gradually stir in the lemon juice until the mixture thickly coats the back of a spoon. Divide evenly between 3 bowls. Add a very little blue food colour to the first bowl and mix until you achieve the desired shade. Cover the bowl with clingfilm to prevent it drying out. Repeat the process with the other 2 bowls, using the yellow and pink food colours.

Pour 1 tsp icing on every cake, using each colour on a third of the batch, gently easing it over with the back of a spoon so it spreads to the edges. Allow to set for 2–3 hours.

Divide the sugarpaste into 3 and colour a third pale pink (see p11), then seal in a polythene food bag at room temperature. Repeat with the other 2 parts of the sugarpaste, colouring one pale blue and the other pale yellow. Roll out to about 2mm thick on a board dusted with a little icing sugar. Stamp out the blossoms and butterflies and allow to dry for a few hours. It is best to prop up the butterflies' wings with skewers or pencils as they dry, so they set as if in flight.

Using the royal icing, stick the blossoms and butterflies to the cakes. Be quite random, so each cake is unique. As a final touch, pipe dots on to each cake and centres into every blossom. Arrange on a cake stand.

MAKES ABOUT 80

1 x Very Lemony Crunch Cake batter (see p31)

80 petit four paper cases
500g icing sugar, sifted, plus more to dust
5–6 tbsp lemon juice
blue food colour
yellow food colour
pink (or red) food colour
100g white sugarpaste
set of 3 blossom cutters (5mm, 10mm and 15mm)
15mm-wide butterfly cutter
60g bag white royal icing, No. 1 nozzle

TO BAKE see: Very Lemony Crunch Cake, p31

christmas gifts

These are perfect as a token edible gift, especially for someone living alone, or for Christmas fairs or teachers' presents. Cut little square gifts from a large cake if you prefer, but here I cook them in baked bean cans. The batter comes to no harm waiting around for an hour or 2, as it will need to be cooked in batches unless you are very fond of baked beans and have 22 empty cans…

Line all the baked bean cans very carefully. They each need to be buttered and their bases and sides lined with baking parchment. Make sure you leave 1cm of parchment higher than the sides of the tin, to make the cakes easier to remove.

Preheat the oven to 140ºC/fan 130ºC/275ºF/gas mark 1. Fill each tin with about 100g of the batter and place them on baking sheets. Bake for 45–50 minutes or until a skewer inserted into the centre comes out clean. Leave to cool for 15 minutes, then turn out on to a wire rack until completely cold. Sprinkle each cake with a little of the rum.

Place the jam and rum for glazing in a small pan. Bring to the boil, then sieve. Dab a little into the centre of each board, place a cake on, then brush a little more all over the tops and sides.

Dust a rolling pin and work surface with icing sugar and roll out about 100g of marzipan to 5mm thick. Lift on to a cake, gently press it to the sides, then cut away the excess. It's important that the marzipan comes right down to the board all around the cake to seal in moisture. Repeat until all the cakes are covered. Leave to dry overnight.

Cut 30cm lengths of ribbon and wrap around some of the cakes, sticking it in place at the back with a little royal icing. Twist raffia around other cakes and tie with a knot.

It is more fun to decorate each cake slightly differently, using a sprig of artificial berries, cinnamon sticks, dried orange slices or star anise flowers. Use the royal icing to 'glue' them into place. Tie up the little cakes in individual cellophane bags (see p202) - or a piece of cellophane cut from a sheet - and finish with a ribbon or a gift tag.

MAKES 22

1 x Tropical Fruit Cake batter (see p44)

butter, for the cans
2–3 tbsp rum, plus 6 tbsp for the glaze
9 tbsp apricot jam
22 x 10cm round thin cake boards
icing sugar, to dust
2kg marzipan (see p138)
6.5m ribbons or raffia
60g bag white royal icing
selection of artificial berries, cinnamon sticks, dried orange slices and star anise flowers

TO BAKE see: Tropical Fruit Cake, p44

melting snowmen

Not everyone wants to eat fruit cake at Christmas and these are simple enough for children to decorate.

Place the cases into 2 fairy cake trays. Pack the cake mixture into the cases so that each is slightly domed and place in the refrigerator to set.

To make the snowmen's heads, roll 20 balls of white sugarpaste (each about the size of a cherry). Dust a work top and rolling pin with icing sugar and roll out the remaining sugarpaste to 5mm thick. Using the cutter, cut out 20 circles. Place 1 on to each cake and smooth into place. Using the white royal icing, stick a snowman's head on to each cake. Allow to dry for a few hours.

Pipe 2 black eyes and a red nose on to each snowman, then stick on 2 mini bean buttons. Finish by twisting a length of sweet around the neck of each snowman, holding in place with a little more royal icing.

MAKES 20 FAIRY CAKES

1 x Surprise Fridge Cake mixture (see p56)

20 foil fairy cake cases
600g white sugarpaste
icing sugar, to dust
6cm round cutter
60g bag white royal icing
60g bag black royal icing
30g bag red royal icing
40 mini chocolate beans
assorted strands, laces and long striped sweets

TO BAKE see: Surprise Fridge Cake, p56

fruit cake fairy cakes

A batch of these make a lovely display on a cake stand at Christmas, or packed into a box as a gift and wrapped in ribbon. They're also vegan.

Preheat the oven to 140°C/fan 130°C/275°F/gas mark 1. Place the fairy cake cases into 3 trays if you have them (or bake in batches) and divide the cake mixture between them. Bake for about 1 hour, or until they spring back to the touch. Cool on a wire rack.

Gently warm the jam in a small pan, then sieve. Brush it over the cakes. Decorate each cake with 3 pecans, 4 almonds and 4 half-cherries. Place the icing sugar in a bowl and gradually add the rum, until you achieve a piping consistency, adding 1 tsp water if necessary. Place in a piping bag, snip the end and drizzle over the cakes.

Arrange on a cake stand or pack into a gift box.

MAKES 34

1 x Vegan Fruit Cake batter
  (see p52)

34 fairy cake cases
8 tbsp apricot jam
102 pecans
136 whole blanched almonds
68 glacé cherries, halved
150g icing sugar, sifted
2–2½ tbsp rum
large piping bag

TO BAKE see: Vegan Fruit Cake, p52

biscuits

iced, layered shortbread

Try lots of fillings. Why not lemon curd, chocolate nut spread or dulce de leche? The cut-out centres in different shapes could be turned into mini biscuits, or re-rolled.

Preheat the oven to 170°C/fan 160°C/350°F/gas mark 3½.

On a floured board, roll the dough out to about 3mm thick and, using the 6.5cm round cutter, cut 40 shortbreads. Cut a central shape – round, heart, star or blossom – from the centre of half the batch, using the smaller cutters. If they are to be frozen, lay the raw biscuits now between sheets of baking parchment in a freezer container. They will need to be defrosted for 1 hour before baking.

Put the shortbreads on 2 baking sheets lined with baking parchment. Cook for 12–15 minutes. (You may need to bake them in batches.) Cool on the baking sheets, then carefully transfer to a wire rack with a palette knife. Leave until completely cold.

Drizzle the royal icing backwards and forwards over the surfaces of all the shortbreads with cut-out centres. Allow to dry.

Spread your chosen filling on to all the other shortbreads, and sandwich together with the iced top layers.

MAKES 40 BISCUITS, 20 WHEN SANDWICHED TOGETHER

1 x Classic Shortbread dough (see p74)

plain flour, to dust
6.5cm round metal cutter
2.5cm round cutter
2.5cm heart cutter (optional)
2.5cm star cutter (optional)
2.5cm blossom (optional)
60g bag white royal icing
2 tsp per biscuit strawberry jam, chocolate spread, lemon curd or dulce de leche

TO BAKE see: Classic Shortbread, p74

doily biscuits

Paper doilies appeared many, many years ago as a cheaper alternative to the crocheted linen used by the aristocracy as far back as the 17th century. By the 1950s, they had become a symbol of upward mobility; no afternoon tea with the vicar would be complete without them! With our current interest in all things retro, they have found a resurgence. These are fun to make; use the tiniest cutters you can find.

Roll out the biscuit dough to about 3mm thick. It is quite sticky, so dust both the work top and rolling pin with flour and chill it every now and then to firm up if necessary. Once rolled, rest it in the refrigerator before cutting out shapes. Cut out 30 heart shapes. At this point, you could lay the biscuits very carefully on to baking parchment, layer into a freezer container and freeze. They will need to be defrosted for 1 hour before baking.

When ready to bake, preheat the oven to 180°C/fan 170°C/350°F/ gas mark 4. Lay the biscuits out on baking parchment and cut shapes from each with the tiny cutters. Using a fine skewer, pierce tiny holes in the biscuits to form a pattern you like.

Bake for 12–15 minutes until pale gold. Remove from the oven and leave to cool on the trays for a few minutes before very carefully transferring to a wire rack. They will firm up as they cool. Display on a plate or cake stand (with or without a paper doily!).

MAKES 30

1 x Vanilla Butter Biscuits dough
  (see p76)

plain flour, to dust
8cm heart cutter
small cutters (I used tiny
  aspic cutters)

TO BAKE see: Vanilla Butter Biscuits, p76

easter tree decorations

Hang these rabbits, eggs and chicks on a few branches of spring blossom for an instant edible display. Children will enjoy decorating these… and not a chocolate egg in sight!

Preheat the oven to 180ºC/fan 170ºC/350ºF/gas mark 4. Roll out the dough using plenty of flour (it is quite sticky) to about 3–4mm thick. Cut out the biscuits with your chosen cutters and lay on 2 baking sheets lined with baking parchment. Make holes towards the top of each with a skewer for threading through the ribbon. Bake for 12–15 minutes, or until pale gold. Cool on a wire rack, re-forming the ribbon holes with the skewer.

Divide the sugarpaste into 3 and place in separate polythene bags. Leave one white for the rabbits, colour one pale yellow for the chicks and the other pale green for the eggs (see p11).

On a clean work surface dusted with icing sugar, roll out the white sugarpaste to about 2mm thick. Cut out with the rabbit cutter, making as many as you have rabbit biscuits. Pipe a little royal icing on to the biscuit and stick on the sugarpaste rabbit. Make a hole in the sugarpaste in the same place as that on the biscuit for the ribbon. Repeat with the yellow sugarpaste on the chicks and the green for the eggs. Pipe pink dots on the rabbit, an ear and an eye, a pink eye for the chick and yellow patterns on the egg.

Allow the sugarpaste and icing to set overnight. Cut the ribbons into 25cm lengths and thread through each biscuit.

MAKES 24

1 x Vanilla Butter Biscuits dough (see p76)

plain flour, to dust
selection of biscuit cutters (I used a rabbit, an egg and a chick, each 7–8cm long)
700g white sugarpaste
1 pot yellow food colour paste
1 pot green food colour paste
icing sugar, to dust
60g bag white royal icing
60g bag pink royal icing
60g bag yellow royal icing
2m 5mm-wide lilac gingham ribbon
2m 5mm-wide orange gingham ribbon
2m 5mm-wide pink gingham ribbon

TO BAKE see: Vanilla Butter Biscuits, p76

autumn leaves

Damp mists, woolly jumpers and long walks gathering conkers and blackberries, meandering through the rustling leaves: each year I wait in anticipation for this time of year, but you can bake these whenever you want. Leaf shapes are very forgiving to make without a cutter as they are organic shapes. I made a template with plastic. Perfect with afternoon tea following a long walk.

Roll out the dough on a lightly floured surface to about 4mm thick. Place it on a tray and put in the refrigerator for 30 minutes; this makes it far easier to work. Cut through the dough around the leaf templates with a sharp knife and, with the tip, score on the veins of the leaves. Place on baking sheets lined with baking parchment. As you work, preheat the oven to 180°C/fan 170°C/350°F/gas mark 4. If the remaining dough becomes too soft before you get to it, chill to firm it up again. (If it's too soft, it will be impossible to cut.)

Bake for 10–15 minutes; the biscuits will have darkened a little. Remove from the oven and leave for a few minutes, then transfer to a wire rack to cool. They will become crisp.

When cool, dust the leaves with a little gold powder, using the brush.

MAKES 30-40

1 x Gingerbread Biscuits dough
  (see p73)

plain flour, to dust
plastic or cardboard stencils of
  leaves (each about 8cm long),
  or leaf cutters
1 file edible gold powder
small paint brush

TO BAKE see: Gingerbread Biscuits, p73

stained glass
tree decorations

These look stunning on a Christmas tree; the coloured 'glass' glows when lit by lights or candles. The biscuits only last a few days on the tree, so eat them before they soften. Use whatever seasonal cutters you have, though you will need 2 sizes of each shape.

Preheat the oven to 180°C/fan 170°C/350°F/gas mark 4. Crush the boiled sweets (still in their wrappers) by bashing with a rolling pin. First placing all the sweets of the same colour in a polythene bag together means they won't shoot all over the kitchen! Line a couple of baking sheets with baking parchment.

Roll out the dough on a lightly floured surface to about 4mm thick and cut out your chosen shapes with the larger cutters. Using the smaller cutters, cut the appropriate shape out of the middle of each. Pierce a hole with a skewer to thread through a ribbon later. Where you make the hole is important as it will affect the way the biscuit hangs from the tree. Re-roll the dough and repeat until it's all used up. (You may need to chill the dough if it gets too soft during this process.) Bake for about 5 minutes, then remove from the oven.

Place ½–1 crushed sweet in each hole, re-form the ribbon hole if necessary, and return the biscuits to the oven. Bake for a further 5–10 minutes, remove from the oven and re-form the ribbon holes for a final time. Cool on the baking sheets.

Cut the ribbon into 25cm lengths and thread through each biscuit.

MAKES ABOUT 20

1 x Gingerbread Biscuits dough
  (see p73)

15–20 coloured boiled sweets
plain flour, to dust
9cm heart cutter
3.5cm heart cutter
12cm tree cutter
4cm tree cutter
10cm angel cutter
3.5cm angel cutter
13cm snowflake cutter
5cm snowflake cutter
5m narrow ribbon

TO BAKE see: Gingerbread Biscuits, p73

gingerbread mobile

A magical addition to any child's room, or anywhere for that matter. The gingerbreads could be any shape: snowflakes or stars at Christmas, butterflies, hearts, flowers or animals. Use whatever cutters you have, or draw a template.

Preheat the oven to 180°C/fan 170°C/350°F/gas mark 4. Line a baking sheet with baking parchment. Chill the dough, then roll it out to about 4mm thick on a lightly floured surface. Cut out the birds and pierce a hole in each with a skewer to thread through the ribbon later. Where you make the hole is important as it will affect the way the bird hangs. Press in a dragee eye for each bird. Bake for 10–15 minutes. Remove from the oven and re-form the holes with the skewer. Leave to firm up for a few minutes, then transfer to a wire rack to cool. They will become crisp. When cool, stick a dragee eye on to the reverse side of each bird, using a little royal icing.

For the mobile, wind the wider ribbon round and round the hoop, overlapping and securing with a firm knot on the inside of the ring. Wrap the cardboard ring with ribbon too, and tie in the same way.

Cut the remaining wide ribbon into 4 equal lengths. Thread the end of 1 piece through a button and tie it around the hoop with a knot. Repeat with the other 3 lengths of ribbon and 3 more buttons, spacing them out evenly around the hoop. Take the other ends of these 4 ribbons and thread them through the cardboard ring, then through the final button. Knot off neatly.

Take 60mm of the narrow ribbon and loop it, too, through the top button. This will hang the mobile.

Thread more of the narrow ribbon through each gingerbread bird. Hang 2 from the cardboard ring and 5 from the embroidery hoop.

MAKES 15 OR 20 BIRDS;
7 BIRDS MAKE 1 MOBILE

½ x recipe Gingerbread Biscuits
  dough (see p73)

plain flour, to dust
dove cutter (or template)
swallow cutter (or template)
14 green dragees
30g bag white royal icing
reel of 15mm-wide orange ribbon
20cm embroidery hoop
1 cardboard ring from a roll
  of sticky tape
5 green buttons with slots or
  large holes
reel of 5mm-wide orange ribbon

TO BAKE see: Gingerbread Biscuits, p73

25 easy cheats

Almost anything can be a decoration, so make a collection of items as you find them.

1 candles

There is a wonderful selection of candles and candleholders available. And try small church candles or tea lights, too. A cake studded with many different, carefully selected candles looks stunning.

Take special care with candles on cakes as they need to be placed well away from other decorations, especially ribbons or artificial flowers.

2 tea lights

Place in a scooped-out clementine, or make a collar out of sugarpaste. I once made a simple crown with cut-out stars in sugarpaste, moulded into a short cylinder. This went on top of the cake with a tea light in the middle. It glowed in the dark.

3 supermarket shelf

There's no need to rely on mail order specialists. Be creative with the plethora of items you'll find in local shops. I found tiny sugar dragees, piped sugar flowers, crystallised rose and violet petals and little sugar orange and lemon slices.

4 fresh flowers

Choose your favourites and, if they're not edible, remove them before cutting the cake. You can paint the edges of the petals with egg white and dip into clear or coloured glitter (I love to do this with white or deep red roses at Christmas). Place 3 or 5 (they always look better when you use an odd number) of glittering roses on a large cake – it looks amazing.

5 bright paper flowers

It is child's play to make tissue or crêpe paper flowers. Stick a circlet of them on top of a cake.

6 fresh berries and fruit

For an instant, wonderful decoration, paint them with egg white and dip into caster sugar to crystallise (see p107). The addition of a few appropriate leaves - try mint with berries, or bay leaves in winter - adds real impact.

7 sweets and chocolates

Make patterns with them or limit the colour palette; using simply black and white, or red and white. Try monochrome liquorice, black-and-white striped ribbon and a red candle.

8 ribbons, braids and beading

Ribbons are instant decorations and most effective. Wrap them around a cake, layer them, overlay different colours, or pull them into a flower shape.

9 doilies and stencils

A visit to your local cake shop will reveal all sorts. I especially like to use heart-shaped doilies on a heart-shaped cake. On the surface of a very flat cake, place a doily or a stencil (make one yourself, maybe the initials of the recipient) and dust with icing sugar or cocoa powder. Very carefully remove the doily or stencil to reveal an intricate pattern.

10 pile of tiny parcels

Cover little matchboxes with plain or tiny-patterned wrapping paper. Tie them with narrow ribbons and decorate with miniature decorations; try bows or flowers. Pile them on a birthday or Christmas cake.

11 reuse packaging

Keep little boxes, bags, ribbons, tissue paper, even the cellophane bags from greetings cards. Use to package home-made biscuits or little cakes.

12 button biscuits

Use any of my biscuit recipes to make little round biscuits. Pierce 2 or 4 holes in the middle of the raw biscuits to resemble buttonholes, then bake, re-form the holes when they come out of the oven and tie liquorice laces or ribbons through the holes.

13 parcels

A square cake can be an edible gift. Wrap the recipient's favourite cake in sugarpaste. Transform into 'wrapping paper' by drawing with edible pens or food colour, or stick on sweets, sugar flowers or dragees. For Christmas, draw on holly and stick on stars. Tie with ribbon and add a hand-written tag.

14 no time to bake?

Dress up a bought cake. If you buy a sponge cake, make flavoured buttercream (see p9) and layer it or simply spread on top. Decorate with any of the quick ideas on this page. If you buy a fruit cake, add a little liqueur (brandy, rum or Madeira), then decorate with ribbon and fresh flowers. Or buy lots of little cakes, ice with buttercream and pile on an array of sweets. Children would love to make these.

15 buy yourself some time

Keep children quiet for a while by getting them to make small cakes into 'bugs'. Give them some multi-coloured chocolate beans and piping bags of coloured icing from the supermarket. They can make bodies with the sweets and pipe on legs and faces.

16 mind the gap

If someone has pinched a slice from a whole cake (especially if it was you), disguise the crime. Slice all the cake, space the slices out and top each with a decoration, or cover each slice with glacé icing.

17 edible pens

A marvellous invention. Buy them from any cake shop. You can draw anything on to a sugarpaste-coated cake, from simple patterns to intricate pictures, in a range of colours. Make sure the sugarpaste is dry first; leave it for at least 24 hours.

christmas quick fixes

18 decorative lights

Instantly enliven a cake with a set of widely available battery-operated Christmas lights. Twist them around the side of a cake, or among crystallised fruits or red berries.

19 make a relief

Cover the cake in marzipan and icing and allow to dry overnight. Then take a cutter of your choice - a large star or tree is very effective - and use it to cut through the icing layer. Remove the cut-out icing. Brush the exposed marzipan with a little melted apricot jam and fill the shape with tiny dragees.

20 seasonal flowers

Cut a polystyrene cup down by half, fill with a piece of moistened oasis and pack in holly and berry sprigs and other seasonal leaves to make a dramatic arrangement. Dust heavily with icing sugar 'snow' and finish with a sprinkle of clear glitter.

21 church candles

Arrange a thick, stubby church candle, a fresh full-blown red rose and a bundle of cinnamon sticks tied with raffia on top of a plain white iced cake.

22 decorate with sweets

Make a stocking, star or tree shape with small sweets, such as mini chocolate beans or jelly beans. Be inspired by my Mosaic Cake (see p90).

23 crystallised fruits

These are widely available during the festive period. Take a fruit cake covered in marzipan - or fully iced if you prefer - and make a pile of crystallised fruits in the centre. Tuck in a few fresh bay leaves (warn your guests these are inedible!) and, if you like, add a touch of gold leaf to the leaves (see p68), slightly dampening the leaves by sprinkling with water first.

24 artificial berries

Take branches of red berries and twist them into a circle the same diameter as a plain white iced cake. Place the wreath on the cake and finish with a broad, deep red ribbon.

25 gingerbread cutters

Buy a few cutters - maybe a gingerbread man, a heart, a tree or star - and use them to make a batch of my Gingerbread Biscuits (see p73). Wash the cutters and layer 3 or 4 of the biscuits inside. Place into a bag (see tip 11, opposite) with a hand-written copy of the recipe, and tie with ribbon.

index

suppliers list

cake and sugarcraft products

Jane Asher
www.janeasher.com
020 7584 6177

Squires Kitchen
www.squires-shop.com
0845 225 5671

ribbons, braids, feathers, artificial birds, butterflies

V V Rouleaux
www.vvrouleaux.com
020 7224 5179

raffia, in a rainbow of colours

Nutscene Direct
www.nutscenedirect.com
01307 468 589

gold leaf

Gold Leaf Supplies
www.goldleafsupplies.co.uk
01656 720 566

vintage and modern kitchen accessories, including glass cake stands

www.re-foundobjects.com
01434 634 567

twin cherry sweets (see p95)

www.originalcandyco.com
01285 711 227

EDITORIAL DIRECTOR Anne Furniss
CREATIVE DIRECTOR Helen Lewis
PROJECT EDITOR Lucy Bannell
DESIGNER Claire Peters
PHOTOGRAPHER Laura Hynd
STYLIST Rachel Jones
PRODUCTION DIRECTOR Vincent Smith
PRODUCTION CONTROLLER Aysun Hughes

First published in 2010 by
Quadrille Publishing Limited
Alhambra House
27-31 Charing Cross Road
London WC2H 0LS
www.quadrille.co.uk

Text © 2010 Fiona Cairns
Photographs © 2010 Laura Hynd
Design and layout © 2010
Quadrille Publishing Limited

The rights of the author have been
asserted. All rights reserved. No part
of this book may be reproduced, stored
in a retrieval system or transmitted in
any form or by any means, electronic,
electrostatic, magnetic tape, mechanical,
photocopying, recording or otherwise,
without the prior permission in writing
of the publisher.

Cataloguing in Publication Data: a
catalogue record for this book is available
from the British Library.

ISBN 978 184400 818 6

Printed in China

credits

p23 pink floral fabric, p25 floral fabric, p29 blue-and-white-striped fabric, p63 spotty and fine-stripe fabrics, p70 colourful floral fabric, p91 white embroidered fabric, p142 white fabric on table, all Cloth House (www.clothhouse.co.uk); p42 floral fabric (design: Mirande), p83 floral fabric (design: Rosanna) and p145 embroidered spot fabric (design: Carreg), all Sanderson (www.sanderson-uk.com, 0844 543 9500); p77 floral silk fabric (design: Rosamund Celadon), Designers Guild (www.designersguild.com, 020 7893 7400); p142 wallpaper (design: Mandara), Osborne & Little (www.osborneandlittle.com)

The word 'acknowledgement' seems so inadequate. Creating a book is a collective process, and I would like to thank so many people.

Firstly my agent Heather Holden-Brown and lovely Elly James for all your patience. Special thanks to Anne Furniss at Quadrille for your faith in me and giving me this amazing opportunity. To my gentle, encouraging editor Lucy Bannell, it has been a great privilege working with you. To Laura Hynd for beautiful, calming photographs. To Claire Peters for wonderful design and Rachel Jones for sensitive styling.

To my old friend Jacqui Pickles, the best cook I know, for your help with development of the most delicious recipes and your work on testing others. Thank you. Without your flair, advice and constructive criticism this book wouldn't be what it is.

To Rachel Eardley. Your talent is exceptional and your creativity knows no bounds. I cannot thank you enough for all your inspiration and help on the book, quite apart from filling in for me at work as well!

I would like to thank Chris Adams, my dear friend, baker and plantswoman extraordinaire. Thank you for your generosity, advice and help (most especially for your exquisite crystallised flowers).

No less gratitude goes to all at the Bakery, both past and present. We are blessed with an exceptional team led by Kishore. Special thanks to Mary Doody (your roses are the best!), Diane Pallett, Angela Withers and Kasia Skotnicka-Tkacz.

Anna Tyler. Your enthusiasm and sheer hard work in the kitchen has been extraordinary and has made this so much easier. I cannot thank you enough. To your wonderful mother Joan for all her recipe testing and wise comments and to Kiki Everard, Amanda Taylor and Eleanor Kilpatrick. David Marshall-Cook and John Moore, thank you for creating Christmas and dappled light respectively! To David Trumper at Jane Asher and Jade Johnston at the Kitchen Range Cookshop in Market Harborough, for your patience. Many, many thanks to Marina Hill for her typing with such speed and efficiency.

I thank my mother for encouraging me to bake at a young age, with rather varying results! Thank you to Lyn Hall, who years ago set me on my way and first taught me the meaning of excellence.

Last, but most definitely not least, to Kishore for running the business so brilliantly and for being my most valued critic! And to my children, Hari and Tara, who endured months of disruption. Sometimes banned from the kitchen and (mostly) uncomplaining, this would not have been possible without you. Thank you.